Praise for Love ~~~~~ *from Poland*

"*Love Letters from Poland*—this story of one woman's spiritual growth is mesmerizing, encouraging, and inspiring because it is real and authentic. The heartfelt expression of the details of her spiritual growth is a rarity today, but as her understanding opens she shares with transparent honesty using colorful images, examples, analogies, metaphors, and word pictures. It is refreshing to read such an open revelation in which most readers will relate more often than not—and appreciate Sarah's ability to document her journey."

-Tom Ziglar, CEO, Zig Ziglar Corporation

"*Love Letters from Poland* touches your heart instantly. Sarah's voice travels quickly into your spirit and fills it with love, hope, and a reminder to always seek God. Her words quickly prove how great inviting God into your daily life can be. If you are a Christian who knows this, you will feel convicted—in a way that will only bring you closer to him. If you are feeling lonely or sad, this book will give you faith that you are not alone—and are loved despite any insecurities you may have."

-Jazmin Richie, business consultant and podcast host of "REV foodservice Podcast"

"*Love Letters from Poland,* if you allow it, will take you on a beautiful journey back home. Back to a place of true rest in His luxurious love, that will quench your thirsty heart."

-Joanna Jezierska

"I think most people have experienced some sort of trauma and hardship in their lives. While everyone's experience is different, there is always a common thread of hurt, shame, and desperation that oddly unites us. Reading Sarah's story has echoed my own fears and pain from my past, yet her raw and honest words have brought peace and hope that can only come from the Father. A beautifully written testimony to God's unfailing love."

-Molly Dunn

"What a beautiful and intimate journey Sarah takes us through. Her story challenges you to see yourself as our Creator does - flawless and loved. You will want to read this in one sitting!"

-Lorin Stoeckle, CPA and health/wellness coach

"Sarah's story is a beautiful testimony of God's redemption. God loves to take the things that were meant to drag us down and turn them into the things that bring him the most glory. He takes the broken pieces of our hearts and lives and puts them back together in such a beautiful way- all because he loves us and wants us to shine!"

-Sarah Linn, Kids Pastor, Mountainbrook Church

Love Letters from Poland

An Unexpected Memoir and
Freedom
Song of a Broken Heart Restored

SARAH DE ORLANDO

Unless otherwise noted, Scripture quotations are taken from the Holy Bible, New
International Version®, NIV®. Copyright © 1973, 1978, 1984, 2011 by Biblia,
Inc. ® Used by permission of Zondervan. All rights reserved worldwide. www.
Zondervan.com. The "NIV" and "New International Version" are trademarks
registered in the United States Patent and Trademark Office by Biblia Inc.®

Scripture quotations marked CSB are from The Christian Standard
Bible, copyright ©2017 by Holman Bible Publishers. Used by
permission. Christian Standard Bible ® and CSB ® are federally registered
trademarks of Holman Bible Publishers, all rights reserved.

Scripture quotations marked NLT are from The Holy Bible, New Living Translation,
copyright © 1996, 2004, 2015 by Tyndale House Foundation. Used by permission
of Tyndale House Publishers, Inc., Carol Stream, Illinois 60188. All rights reserved.

Scripture quotations marked NASB are from the New American Standard
Bible Copyright © 1960, 1962, 1963, 1968, 1971, 1972, 1973, 1975,
1977, 1995 by The Lockman Foundation. Used by permission of The
Lockman Foundation, La Habra, Calif. All rights reserved.

Hardcover ISBN: 978-1-64184-512-0
Paperback ISBN: 978-1-64184-513-7
eBook ISBN: 978-1-64184-514-4

Library of Congress Control Number: 2020923477

The Internet addresses in this book are accurate at the time of publication. They
are provided as a resource. Sarah de Orlando does not endorse them or vouch for
their content, services, or permanence of these sites beyond the life of this book.

To protect the privacy of many of the people in this
memoir some names have been changed.

Photography:
Front Cover: by Free-Photos at www.Pixabay.com
Back Cover Portrait: Katie Pepi, www.poppyandvinevisual.com

Cover Design: JETLAUNCH, www.jetlaunch.com

Dedication

To my daughter, Annabelle Grace.

My sweet Bug, and the generations to come from our family: may you continue the legacy of passionately pursuing Jesus' heart, rooted in love, and filled in abundance with the fullness of God. You are such a precious gift from our Heavenly Father. Love you forever.

For this reason, I kneel before the Father, from whom every family in heaven and on earth derives its name. I pray that out of his glorious riches he may strengthen you with power through his Spirit in your inner being, so that Christ may dwell in your hearts through faith. And I pray that you, being rooted and established in love, may have power together with all the Lord's holy people, to grasp how wide and long and high and deep is the love of Christ, and to know this love that surpasses knowledge—that you may be filled to the measure of all the fullness of God.
Ephesians 3:14-19

Table of Contents

Author's Note

This is a work of nonfiction. The details of experiences and events have been faithfully recounted to the best of my ability. Some names have been changed to protect the anonymity of the individuals involved. Although I vividly recall many of these events and conversations, some dialogue may not be told word-for-word but is shared to communicate the sentiment and meaning behind the event.

Foreword

Sarah's story is one of profound change, of finding freedom from abuse, shame, and fear by meeting and experiencing the extravagant love of God. Sarah isn't interested in getting you to do anything outside yourself, like more routines or goals or contorting yourself to meet some ideal, because her story is of a God whose desire is to come close, to draw out what is longing to be free, loved, and seen. Sarah's story is a story of God walking among us, patiently, to help us wake up to our beloved humanity.

The contours of your own story may differ, or maybe you have not walked the road of faith in anything or anyone. This is still a great book for anyone looking for change. Maybe you've lost a bit of hope in the possibility that life can be different, vibrant, and rid of the ghosts of your past. Or maybe you are on a different path but could use encouragement to keep going. This is a great read and written with you in mind.

-Megan Thomas

Preface

The orange life jacket hugged my small torso. I squinted through the afternoon sun to watch Dad. My heart was still as we went along on our daddy-daughter adventure. He wore his Volkswagen t-shirt and paddled our canoe as an occasional cigarette dangled from his lips. The paddle went swiftly into the water, then up, dribbling and leaving tiny whirlpools behind. I daydreamed as we passed banks of pines, soaking in the sights and sounds of peace. Thick exposed roots clung to granite-making small hideaways for critters-before the trees drank deeply from the current. It struck me as odd in my seven-year-old mind that they didn't crash into the water.

No one told me the waters of life would get rough, or I would lose sight of the shore for some time. But it happened. Things beyond my control tried to drown my hope and purpose for life. Childhood trauma and depression have an awful way of changing the current, and I was swept away by both. I tried to paddle myself to shore. I tried to find happiness and freedom from my emptiness. But nothing anchored me for long.

One day drifting aimlessly along with no one steering my heart, the Lord would scoop me up. He saw me as I floundered along through rough, choppy waters, and sharp rocks of trials. Scars marred my soul as I searched for purpose. But he would set me on the firm rock of his love and let me take root. From the depths, he called me out and freed me to stand tall knowing who I was created to be.

I wrote this book for the broken and hurting, those feeling unworthy and unloved—especially for my aching soul. Deep down, below my conscious yearnings, I needed restoration and freedom. Jesus met me and healed me in Poland. Now I am bravely sharing my encounter on these pages. I have been wrecked by his love over and over again, as I have chosen to accept and walk in the lavish grace of his forgiveness.

This is the freedom song of my life, the story of his love for me.

I pray you may reflect on your story and have renewed hope. Get to know Jesus, friend. He longs to love you and redeem the most broken, painful parts of your life too.

Poland was a powerful eight months of my life when I was overwhelmed by God's deep love for me. He chased me, called me, and scooped me up in his arms, and said, "you're mine, my daughter." The Lord healed me and set a new burning purpose in my heart and trajectory for my life—one of hope, power, wisdom, joy, and especially his profound love for me.

I am giving you a gift from my heart—the heart God gave me, so I may share his love with you. Especially *you*. I believe God led you to this book, and he wants to speak to you. Through many prayers and tears, God humbly prepared me to share my story with you, free from fear and shame of my past. It is terrifying to be so open about my past and let you see where I've been—abused, clinically depressed, ashamed, and rejected. But then, I hope you see where I stand now—rooted in love, healed, and empowered. I'm still a flawed woman but now I see God's goodness woven throughout my life and proclaim this story because it is the one he created for me. My identity is not found in what I've done or what has been done to me. Instead, I see myself in light of his unshakable character and forgiveness, so I can rest in the name he gave me: his beloved.

I sought the Lord, and he answered me; he delivered me from all my fears. Those who look to him are radiant; their faces are never covered in shame. Psalm 34:4-5

Sarah de Orlando
October 2020
San Luis Obispo, CA, USA

March 19, 2016
Chelmsford, Massachusetts

Goodbye, Hello

CHAPTER 1

My journey to Poland and the changed life I would experience was climactic in every way. I encountered a mountain of newness physically, emotionally, spiritually as I got to know Jesus, not by a shadow, but face to face. It was a clash of past and present, a spiritual awakening setting more in motion for my life than I ever thought possible.

To know where you are going, you must get acquainted with where you've been. If the past you come from is rife with abuse, resulting in trauma, those experiences we wish never happened, sometimes hindsight is the only worthy guide. We can only process some things in the comfort of time. But God was laying the groundwork, even when I didn't know it. As an adult, I came to experience the living God, but only by returning to the beginning.

I warmed up in my bathrobe sipping black coffee on a dreary morning, a gray dead Earth lay outside my window. Low clouds hung over our apartment by the train tracks. Trees stood bare and songbirds held their breath.

GOODBYE, HELLO

I journaled in my rocker, pouring ink onto the pages, trying to find clarity amid my chaotic thoughts. *Could I handle being apart from Andrés for the next eight months? Was I fit for my new job? What would my new normal be like? Would I make friends? Would God sustain me?*

When I wrote that morning, I had dedicated the last eight years to my engineering career, six in school, and the remainder working. The journey from the dreams and grandeur of my childhood aspirations to actually becoming an engineer are worlds apart, but it put me on an imperfectly perfect path to where my real life began.

The squish of clay and the swish of a paintbrush were my melodies as a child. Creating masterpieces on rainy days, snow days, and all the other days I wasn't trapped in school. "Mommy, I want to be an artist when I grow up!" My mom would smile, put her hand on my head, and say something like, "Maybe, we'll see." Somehow I began believing it was impractical to make art and get paid for it, maybe it was the subtle tones I perceived, or perhaps my older brothers told me about some rich tech guru named Bill Gates. Regardless, I crumbled up my dream of being an artist and threw it in the garbage before I completed elementary school. The ever-responsible child, I had to figure out something more stable to make a living.

My next dream: becoming an architect. Boston's skyline was my inspiration. Field trips to the big city as I peered through the bus windows captured my heart. The bigger the building, the bigger my accolades, I reasoned. Vibrant city life contrasted starkly with my small hometown in New Hampshire. Pursuing architecture was my dream throughout high school. My life plan included being good at math and science, with Spanish, band, and English classes peppered in. I scooped ice cream in a 50's style boutique shop and dreamed of a vibrant career between mopping the checkered floors and ringing up orders.

However, my vision was dashed as I looked at college application requirements. A portfolio of my artwork - I had never considered needing such a thing and only took one art class in high school. Scurrying, I found my plan B: architectural engineering. Then I was back on track to achieve awesomeness and get out of my depressing hometown.

College applications were sent. I received rejection letter after rejection letter in my mailbox. Some schools didn't even send a letter - only a disappointing, conciliatory email. Looking back, I give myself grace. I had been aggressive with my choices which included prestigious places like California Institute of Technology, Massachusetts Institute of Technology, and Cornell University. As salutatorian of my high school class of 78 students, I thought I had a better chance than most. Alas, Clarkson University in middle-of-nowhere upstate New York accepted me. They did not have an architecture program, nor an architectural engineering program. I settled for civil engineering. I could design beautiful bridges spanning vast waters. I could help people with my elegant solutions and put my excellent mathematical skills to use. *I could still be somebody.*

Freshman year of college was academically challenging. I studied in groups to glean from others instead of putting in a lot of hard work to understand myself. Excellent grades in high school came to me so easily, what happened to me? Changing my major never occurred to me; most of my college friends were engineers too, we were just in the grind. I couldn't waste this brain of mine and ruin the plan I had created. I wasn't a quitter. Coming into sophomore year, I learned I *was* capable of studying and achieving good grades as I found a better support network and asked for help. But something still didn't quite click. During many of my upper-level engineering classes, I took notes but daydreamed about my sweetheart, Andrés. *Once I get an exciting job*, I thought, *I'll be able to focus and thrive.* Andrés asked me to marry him on Halloween of my senior year of college. It was a surprise to me and not part of my plan to get married so young, but it felt right. My future looked weird if I tried imagining being with anyone else. Exactly two months later, my grandpa walked me down the aisle in the cozy Adirondack lodge nestled in the pines as tears of joy stung my eyes.

When we graduated, Andrés and I had a brief stint living in Los Angeles, then we moved to Massachusetts. He began working and I went back to school for a graduate degree. In the summer of 2012, I had a great engineering internship and made life-long friends with my mentor and project manager, Matt. That fall I began a rigorous master's program at Northeastern University. But even before I set foot on campus in a sea of 16,000+ other students, I realized I needed something else in my heart to weather the overwhelming pressure to perform and keep everyone happy. I decided to try talking to God and see if he could help calm my strong emotions and dull the pain of my depression. I remember my mom always reading Our Daily Bread devotions. I got one and put it in my backpack. What could it hurt to try reading the scripture and an inspiring story occasionally? It felt safe, no one would need to know what I was reading.

I had newfound peace and I was absorbed in the learning environment of graduate school in the bustling city. My Advanced Steel Design professor would say, "It's a beautiful day to derive," and then launch into his lecture. Burning the midnight oil, I studied hard to receive B's and an occasional A. I was proud and ready to take on the world of structural engineering when graduation arrived. Elated, I got my first "big girl" job at AECOM just outside of Boston. I was ready for my passion to take flight in the freedom of adulthood.

I loved the idea of AECOM—it was an 80,000+ employee, international engineering behemoth. I had dreams of working on their megaprojects, traveling the world, and eventually leading large multi-disciplinary teams to success. Less than two years into my career, an opportunity in Poland came to be.

Christianity was part of the fabric of my family when I was a child and we frequently attended a non-denominational church. Like a silent parade of ducklings, my family of seven filed into the sanctuary five minutes late most Sunday mornings. But the music and messages didn't click for me. I just doodled pictures of me dancing on stages as a beautiful ballerina and thought the trombone sounded like musical farts. God's heart seemed to love everyone else but me. I felt horrible when I was a bad girl and felt barely "good enough" the rest of the time. I didn't belong anywhere and seemed to float along and be amicable and helpful.

As an introvert, I thought I had to be someone else to be seen. Like there was something wrong with my personality and that's why I had few friends. I was a good student and appreciated affirmations from my teachers. Quickly, I adopted the name "teacher's pet," "brown-noser," and "over-achiever" from my classmates as my heart ached to be seen. My desire to feel worthy of being known and loved drove me to achieve many of my academic successes. I longed for approval with everything I did, it was how I clung to glimpses of love.

My job title was critical to my identity. As a child, you are asked, "What do you want to be when you grow up?" When you are plopped into adulthood, the story changes slightly but implies heavy expectations, "What do you do?" No longer are we given permission to wonder. We're supposed to know and already be doing it. Engineering was my only choice. I felt pride well up when telling others I was somebody important: an engineer. I told myself so many times, I truly believed it was my life calling. I liked getting outside to inspect corroded steel beams and writing technical reports. But mostly, I liked encouraging and listening to my coworkers and clients.

I didn't realize God was nudging me along the right path. He was closing one door, but opening another throughout my exploration of my vocation, and moving me in baby steps toward trusting his heart.

Growing up, my mom stayed at home and my dad was an auto mechanic; his salary disappeared quickly to house, feed, and clothe so many people. I recall my mom telling me, "Pick any cereal you want as long as it's less than $1.99/lb." I never felt a lack or noticed their worry as a child, but I didn't have a complete grasp on how to manage my own money as a young adult either.

After high school, private college price tags weren't scary for me, I had over half my college paid for by generous scholarships. Credit cards didn't seem like a bad idea either to bridge the gap for fun money. I thought I was intelligent and would soon have a well-paid engineering job. But six months after graduation, the grace period of my loans ended, and Andrés and I had ugly bills to pay. We couldn't, so we deferred. I continued to buy groceries on credit at Trader Joe's and shop at Target aimlessly seeking those fleeting feel-good mood boosts from my purchases. Grad school ended, and so did my final grace period. The payments were ridiculous, but with my new job, we could wink, nod, stand on one foot, and *sort of* cover our expenses.

In early 2015, I felt a desire to seek God's wisdom in the Bible about how to handle our money. He said, "Do you trust me?" Then I stumbled upon a podcast with Dave Ramsey's funny spiel about how couples relate to money. I was hooked. "Conveniently" I cornered Andrés in the car and had him listen. He laughed. I think he even *liked* it. It lit a spark; he Googled Ramsey and found his podcast.

Andrés listened to the Dave Ramsey Show podcast non-stop. He ordered his book, *The Total Money Makeover*, and read it in a few days. In less than a month, we enrolled in Financial Peace University (FPU).

We came face to face with an ugly fact. We were drowning.

$256,000.00 in debt.

Our lives were turned upside-down when we had to list all our debts. The poor FPU coordinator, when tallying up the total class debt, said, "I think someone included their mortgage in their debt total..." in his thick Massachusetts accent.

Nope. That was us. (As we sheepishly nodded at our coordinator, Joe). I always liked being top of the class, but this was a new level.

Between the two of us, we had three private school degrees, two cars, and several credit cards. With lofty dreams of saving for a house and no specific plan for how to make progress, we were grasping at the wind. We were scraping by to make the $2,000 minimum monthly payments on our debt. No wonder God was leading us toward this program.

By the time I left for Poland, less than a year later, we had already paid off over $40,000. Our fire was stoked and our trust in God had rapidly grown. We had seen him move and provide for us. "God math" is what we called it; on paper, we thought we had so much, but then God honored our diligence and multiplied it. With our momentum, I was full of hope going to Poland. I knew we would make a tremendous impact on our debt payoff with favorable financial incentives.

God was freeing us from debt and showing us his heart as a good Father - one who wanted to abundantly meet our needs. I didn't yet know the next right thing God would do for me was free me from the prison of my depression, pain from childhood trauma, neglect, and limiting beliefs. Jesus knew I would fall apart, safely into his loving arms.

In March of 2016, Słupsk (pronounced Swoopsk), a humble working city in northern Poland became my new temporary home. I worked as an engineer on a high-profile military construction site. I always had a heart to travel and for humanitarian work. Within two years after graduation, I had applied for post-earthquake structural assessment work in Nepal and Haiti. However, to my disappointment, I wasn't selected for either team.

When I heard about the Poland assignment, I was eavesdropping as a project manager pitched the idea to a coworker. "So, what do you think about Poland?... Interested in an on-site construction services assignment for a year?", he inquired with his Boston accent. It was just a week or two before Christmas.

Europe was always on my bucket list but never Poland specifically. It didn't have the allure of rolling hills and fruitful vineyards, beautiful Mediterranean beaches, or exquisite food. Poland was undervalued, an undiscovered gem with a marred history.

I stood up and peered over my festive cube wall at my colleague. "Ha, good luck with that!" I teased. He chuckled as he leaned back, arms behind his head, "I'm not going there!"

I don't remember exactly when I stopped thinking the assignment was a joke. Slowly, I began pondering some pros and cons. I *was* eager to travel and get more independent work experience. "Who cares if it isn't as exotic as Nepal?", I reasoned with myself. "So what if I'm not doing disaster aid relief?" And so, I chewed on it and prayed about it. I was also motivated by financial incentives. Andrés and I were laser-focused on our robust financial plan and were eager to accelerate progress.

Some coworkers on the project team assuaged me. They said besides it being 2+ hours from a regional airport, it was a quaint community in the beautiful countryside. Also, not to worry, "there is a local mall!" (I hate shopping).

Practically everyone told me I should go except for my grandmothers. They were concerned about me leaving my Andrés for months. "Who would care for him? Who would iron his clothes?" Andrés and I agreed he'd manage with Costco chickens, kale salad, and an unkempt house. My sweet friend, Bre, offered to drop off some meals for Andrés. He joked he wouldn't survive, but then again he also said, "I don't let the truth get in the way of a good story." I *was* the primary caretaker for our house and did most of the shopping and cooking unless I wanted his specialty: oatmeal. But it wasn't that he expected these things. He gladly pitched in when I asked for help, but I enjoyed showing my love by serving him in those ways. Since I grew up as the mature and helpful eldest daughter, taking responsibility for these chores came naturally.

In January 2016, after some negotiations for a lesser assignment term of 8-months instead of 1 or 2 years, I was on the team and going to work in Poland. I had a million things in preparation for my role. My passport was updated, background checks were verified, a military ID was obtained, and I met with the structural team in our Washington D.C. office. Andrés and I even squeezed in a two-week vacation to Ecuador to see his family. Everything happened in rapid-fire.

"Polonia? Eh?" My father-in-law, Domingo, asked as we sat outside hoping a breeze would dance through the palm trees. Belly laughs of the Orlandos' surrounded us with other conversations. "Yeah. Poland. It should be good," I said. He smiled, nodding. Our language barrier left us without much more to say.

Sure, I was hoping to explore Poland and support my country as a civilian, but I was worried about the unknowns I would face on the other side of the Atlantic. I couldn't communicate my feelings with Domingo, because I hadn't been honest with myself. *Just keep moving*, I told myself. I kept pushing forward, stuffing my fears and worries down like the clothing in my suitcase, hoping somehow I'd keep myself zipped up and together.

On the day of my departure, I sat in the stillness of the morning to reflect.

My soul ached for reassurance from the Lord. Like a feather in the wind, I could never settle. My mind was always worrying about or planning for the next thing. Multi-tasking and setting high expectations exhausted me. I was thirsty for lasting peace. But I couldn't grasp how boldly God would answer my prayers as I followed his lead to Poland.

I was saying goodbye to the legalistic, shameful, depressed captivity which had overshadowed most of my life. As I fought against my mind, I felt like a wave tossed in the sea, back and forth, never anchored. But I didn't realize it was an issue, I just kept fighting with myself. My heart churned under self-hatred and hopelessness. "God loves you!" They said, but they didn't know me. No one talks about sexual abuse in the Church.

Until my early twenties, God seemed nonexistent or distant, and as though he only desired my obedience like a strict judge. The Bible, his rule book, was confusing and stressful. I wanted to be a good girl. I wanted to be accepted. But it seemed better to ignore him and find joy and acceptance from people instead.

I didn't believe God could move in miraculous ways in my life. Instead, I thought I just had to obey, keep my head down, and earn a spot in Heaven. It seemed like a one-sided relationship where God didn't have specific hopes and plans for my life. I thought debt was a fact of life and we'd be stuck with our student loans for decades. I thought engineering had to be my career because it paid well, I was decent at it, and had spent too much for those flashy degrees. At the time I couldn't clearly see how God could move me in another direction, after years on this path. My life's trajectory was set, or so I thought.

Below my conscious yearnings, I needed hope. The week before my departure, on the surface, I was worried about derailing our budget because of broken appliances and wasted food.

Rocking back and forth, a raw, heartfelt pray flowed onto the page:

Dear Heavenly Father,

Thank you for being my provider—Yahweh Jireh, you are my source for all things. Our fridge broke this week, and you gave us a cooler, mini-fridge, and ice. You ensured we still had food to eat— plenty of food. You gave me my daily bread, but I still was initially overwhelmed and angry it happened. Forgive me for snapping at Andrés, forgive me for ultimately doubting your promise to provide for us. Despite my sin and doubt, you were faithful and gave us an abundance. Your timing was perfect for the delivery this morning so we both could still lead FPU (Financial Peace University). Grow my trust to see you as my provider—even or especially when it seems illogical from a human perspective.

Lord, thank you for providing this amazing opportunity for me to work in Poland. You had this plan to help us crush debt long before we even recognized we had a debt problem. Previously, we saw the money we earned as ours, not yours. But now we know you've graciously given us these bless-

ings to manage. I can't believe we have this great opportunity to manage even more money for you! Let us contribute unitedly, with you at the center of our mission.

Lord, you know I am scared and worried about the what-ifs, the distance apart, potential failure—send all these thoughts far away from my heart. Let me take them captive and obedient to Christ. They are lies! You tell me to be strong and courageous. Don't be afraid, don't be discouraged; for the LORD my God will be with me wherever I go! That's always true! You are my Yahweh Shammah—the Lord is there. You are always present, listening, leaning in to hear me. Let me turn to you and know you are my banner Yahweh Nissi. You are the banner over my life as I go through battles. I know you are fighting for me. Let me look up to you and have peace and encouragement from this truth.

Lord, thank you for being everything I need. Thank you for your unmerited mercy and grace in my life. Let me live this life in obedience and as a fragrant offering to you. Let others see your glory through me and advance your kingdom.

Let me know you make all things work together for my good and you do it all. Let me give you the reins and credit for the things I do. It's all a blessing from you, my Father.

I am amazed by your lavish love for me.

I love you, Lord, and let my love grow deeper as I grow in knowing you, trusting your promises, and seeing your due honor and glory.

In Jesus' Name,
Amen

But thanks be to God, who always leads us as captives in Christ's triumphal procession and uses us to spread the aroma of the knowledge of him everywhere.
2 Corinthians 2:14

I had limited dreams for my life abroad. I just thought I was going to advance my career, dabble in learning Polish, and make a ton of money to pay off our mountains of debt to impress Dave Ramsey! Forget about joy, freedom from strongholds, and resting in his deep and constant love. Forget about coming face to face with the lover of my soul, Jesus. I found solace knowing I had at least one trip back home secured, only three weeks into my assignment, for my friend's wedding. If I was dying of loneliness and failing at work, I could just curl up under my covers and stay home.

Jesus was knocking on my heart, looking to come in and embrace me as his dearest friend. Would I greet him and open the dark caverns of my heart? Would I let him love me? Not yet. I didn't think I needed love.

Evening came, it poured as Andrés drove me to Logan Airport. We were silent, *was this really happening?* I was

14

locked in, no turning back now. Andrés reached out and gave me a reassuring squeeze. I choked back a flood of emotions.

My mom, sister, Rebekah, and long-time family friend, Judy, (who always told me I was beautiful and should be a model) surprised me to send me off with snacks and love. It was painful to leave, especially to say goodbye to Andrés, and with tears streaming down my face I passed through security. As I reached into my chest pocket to store my passport, a mint green love note emerged in my own tiny script. God's voice stilled the bustling airport around me:

"Have I not commanded you? Be strong and courageous, do not be afraid, do not be discouraged, for the Lord your God will be with you wherever you go." Joshua 1:9

A gulp of water to my parched, anxious soul.

It wasn't unusual for me to scrawl out a verse on a sticky note or margin. They were all over my work cubicle, my nightstand, and stuffed in notebooks. But I never kept them in my pockets until then. The verse was a prompt from my Bible study that morning. I even included it in my prayer, but I didn't believe God was speaking directly to me. There was too much noise in my mind to hear his calm, reassuring voice.

He softly spoke again; I *am with you. Sarah, I am with you.*

Ok, Lord, you now have my attention, my worried heart stilled.

I found my coworkers. We boarded our flight. Thankfully, I was not seated by them; I needed solitude. Of course, my overstuffed bag didn't fit under the seat. Andrés had been gracious, and never breathed a word about my burgeoning luggage. I settled in by the window; the plane barreled down the runway. Accelerating up, Boston's lights faded through the clouds and the dark, calm Atlantic stretched beyond view. I reached back into my pocket and clutched the paper's hope-filled truth.

I am courageous.

I am courageous!

The tears kept coming, but so did a growing peace from within; I was not alone.

As a little girl, my dad would sing to me,
"Sarah is so silly! Silly, silly Sarah."

Spring 2016
Słupsk, Poland

He loves me. He loves me... still?

CHAPTER 2

I sat in a field, green grass swaying in the breeze, only nine years old. Reaching out, I picked a daisy. "He loves me," went one petal, "He loves me not," another petal dropped and so I continued. My heart sank, landing on the latter as the last petal drifted to the Earth. "I'll try another, that one has to be right…" Longingly, I kept plucking and believing I could find what my heart longed for in a field of wildflowers.

Poland was unlike what I expected. It was wet and dark with strange road signs and skinny women smoking cigarettes against buildings. The sound of diesel cars reminded me of childhood when dad would come home in his Volkswagen Rabbit. It gave me some hope. The smell of wood fires hung in the air. Raindrops clung to my neon red North Face and glasses as I explored the small city of Słupsk by foot. I lived a block from a large cemetery where vendors filled the sidewalks. They offered a rainbow of arrangements, signs, and candles for the beloved deceased. My hotel room had a particular aroma, it wasn't bad, but it wasn't quite good. Waking up, I opened my curtains for a perfect view of the sunrise through the barren trees. *Something good must come of this, Lord. I just don't know what. I'm listening.*

Just days after arriving, I was overwhelmed with anxiety about my new work role and intense loneliness being away from Andrés. I didn't have him, or even a new friend to hug. I ached for Andrés' consistency. His even-temper steadied my sensitive heart, and he always wanted to problem solve for me in a calm, practical manner. He offered his critical thinking via Whatsapp, but his words fell flat without a reassuring hug. I craved physical touch; it's how I felt loved, safe, secure.

I believe in a good, loving God, but I also know there is an enemy, the devil. His goal, as scripture warns, is "only to steal and kill and destroy" all of the Lord's good plans.[1] It should have been no surprise to me that I had a big target on my back as the Lord led me to Poland. The enemy was desperately trying to exploit my feelings of isolation and being unloved. Without hesitation, I opened the door like he was an old, trusted friend. He sat down, put up his feet, and spewed out all my inadequacies as I graciously offered tea and believed his stories.

Professionally, I was truly underqualified for the position (but God had protected me from that knowledge until months after my arrival), and I was also a young female in a heavily male-dominated office. I feared they would soon uncover my perceived incompetence. *God may have brought me here,* I thought, *but he won't see me through.* Lies.

Relationally, most of my life I ascribed my value from physical affection and being in relationships. But now I was all alone. I knew I would remain faithful to Andrés, but how would our relationship look with months of separation? Could I bravely explore alone? Grocery shop alone? He had been my partner in everything for the last seven years. Who would I be without him at my side? No one. Lies.

The enemy of our souls has sneaky ways of trapping us within our fears, making us doubt our identities, taking half-truths and twisting them. If you listen long enough, they become believable. How about lies like, "They'd hate me if they knew the real me" or "No one sees me" as you're thrown into a pit of rejection? What about lies like "I'll always be a failure" and "I'm not good enough" as the sur-mounting pressure of life's demands screams at you to quit?

I've been there, friend, buried in a pit of lies, so far from God's truth and love. I've plucked those petals hoping to find love and comfort from controlling situations and grasping at transient things to define me. Riddled with insecurity, I withdrew from others. Bring my fears to light? Never. What if everyone confirmed them?

The lies yell louder as we step out into the unknown. "Change is bad!" Our minds convince us to run back to normal, to numb with distractions, to live small, to not step into the promises God has for us. Somewhere, deep inside our souls, we know we're meant for more. Can we scrape up enough courage to believe we are who God says we are and walk boldly in his truth?

You see, in my broken past, I sought love and approval from boys. From age fourteen, I dated one unhealthy guy to the next until God stopped me in my tracks just weeks before my 20th birthday.

Since I can remember I believed I was worthless: "Full of crap with my brown hair and eyes with my ski-jump nose," as my brothers badgered. It cut deep. My love languages are words of affirmation and physical touch. My mom and I bonded over baking from scratch. Sipping tea, we'd devour our sweet creations still steaming from the heat. Treats were my respite to lift a bad mood. *Feelings? What feelings? I'll just have another tasty cookie*, I told myself.

I'm the middle child of five. Usually, I was a calm, quiet peacekeeper. Unless my siblings bothered me, then my temper flared. When I was hurt, I wanted to lash out and fight back verbally or physically. I had so much pain locked away in my heart. And on the other end—when others were mad, I hunkered down, cleaned, did my homework, and tried to be a good girl. What I didn't understand then was I was suffering from depression and post-traumatic stress from sexual abuse.

Before I even lost my two front teeth, a manipulative girl said she wouldn't be my friend unless I took baths with her and let her touch me. What could I do? Now I understand someone must have hurt her terribly to introduce those ideas in her mind. However, it scarred me with deep shame, and I knew it didn't feel right. But then when other inappropriate things happened in my family, I was desensitized and rationalized it in my mind for several years. When I was 12, I went to a purity retreat at my church and the shame of my past buried me. I was too dirty; who would forgive me? Who would listen? The event was based on a book called "And the Bride Wore White." I could never wear that color.

There was no hope. I had deep shame for what I had done and what had been done to me. I was trying to find connection, to feel accepted and loved. I began spiraling with deep depression when I realized the gravity of it all when I reached adolescence.

I couldn't see the goodness of God's original, good design for sexuality, and loving that part of us. My pain painted a dark smear across any hope for my future. I would always be a dirty outcast. I loathed myself for ruining my entire life. I would never be blameless or pure, I believed. I rationalized others could be freed from shame, but not me. Not my sins. Jesus wasn't enough for what I had done. Pain and sin tainted the picture I had for God's good design. The trauma twisted my view and was turned against me by the enemy. I kept a fortress around my heart, no one would love me if they knew the real me.

Unsurprisingly, I numbed my pain, stuffing it deep within my broken soul. I promised myself I could run far from my past and be a "good" girl. No one would have to know. I felt no one really loved me for me. How could they? I didn't even know myself. But as a teenager, I realized I could date boys to fill the deep voids of my aching soul. I felt seen and heard in relationships—even if many times their motives were shallow. I ruined nice boys; I didn't believe I deserved them. Typically, I got bored or they got needy, I would cheat and then dump them. They seemed too simple and wouldn't understand my pain. Instead, I began gravitating toward those older *bad*-boy types. My first love devastated me when he eventually rejected my heart. I was too immature, I had too much pain. I was too much.

Years too late, a sibling tattled to our dad about my promiscuity when rumors flew through our small town. Dad cornered me, and I brushed him off, "So what?" I shrugged.

He had lost my respect, especially after he disappeared to Mexico for a year without explanation. Who was he to correct me now? Practically an adult, I felt I had to deal with my own emotions and make decisions. My mom kept saying "Be good and just be friends," unaware of the gravity of my suffering. I couldn't tell her and burden her with my problems. She was too wounded picking up the pieces of her own life that my dad had shattered.

I found comfort and value in my life in romantic relationships. I was on cloud nine when I got attention and spiraled into depression and suicidal thoughts when I was rejected.

But now I thank my Papa God for holding me in my darkest times. He protected me from myself and those boys who broke my heart and left, even when I couldn't see it through the pain. I never needed a shot-gun wedding; I wasn't stuck in toxic relationships. Somehow he pulled me together to survive another day and give me small reprieves from my harsh inner voice. Somewhere deep in my soul, I had a glimmer of hope. Friend, I know I couldn't be here telling you the ugliest parts of my story apart from God's persistent love for me.

He knew who my heart needed...

Andrés.

We were born on different continents and years apart. He grew up speaking three languages. I grew up speaking some weird blend of English dialects. For instance, I thought "bob wire" was the poky wire guarding pastures, and I felt elegant calling my mom Mum. Many times Andrés teased me when I had an ah-ha moment about my New England spelling blunders. He would retort, "Isn't English *your* language?!" At least we both had a sense of humor. The Lord created our hearts for each other.

By God's grace, Andrés was unlike anyone I had ever known. He recalls his first impression of me teasingly, "She's cute and I'm going to date her!" After several months of pursuit, I realized he wasn't married nor an overly friendly grad student wanting me to join his Aikido club. He took me out for Moroccan food and a movie. He greeted me with a kiss on the cheek. I grasped his bicep as we crossed the street and he held the door for me. We were like magnets stuck together. We laughed. We told stories. I don't remember anyone else in the restaurant; it was only him. Our first kiss on the threshold of my dormitory still gives me butterflies.

Andrés was caring, loving, hard-working, and smart. He loved his family and called his parents weekly back home in Ecuador. He was tall-ish, dark, and handsome. His laugh echoed through the engineering building, I only needed to pause and listen to locate him. Andrés was also firm and honest and would not put up with emotional manipulation, refusing to engage when I tried to fight unfairly. He challenged me to grow up, and even though we were far from God, the Lord was working in us. Andrés felt safe to me and was the first person I believed *actually* loved me unconditionally. I was dumbfounded. Even when I began to let down my walls and share the horrors of my past, my deepest shames, he kept loving me. God was pulling me in, showing me his tender loving-kindness through Andrés. I was not too dirty or too broken to receive or learn to give love.

I now see God's hand was on our relationship. Even when old lies and insecurities rose, like when my freshman year ex randomly reached out, God cut him off. Andrés and

I were meant to stay together, and we would be loyal. One time, just before we were engaged, I remember God protecting me, protecting us, despite my wayward efforts.

Andrés was in Ecuador to see family and to work on a project for Engineers without Borders. Home alone, I made a lunch date with an ex. However, the morning of, I woke up with a vicious stomach bug, canceled my lunch plans, and even had to reschedule my graduate school exam the same day. I never had that lunch; God didn't let me fall back into old habits of seeking affection in broken places. As I lay in agony on our futon, I realized how terrible my choices had been. I came clean to Andrés over Skype. I feared verbal abuse and anger, but he listened and graciously forgave me for considering it. Our mission as a couple was greater than I could even imagine. God's favor was on us, his love surrounded us… fast forward a few years, when Andrés visited me in Poland for my birthday, we received special encouragement from Pastor Sergio. He told us, "Only God could have brought you two together." Tears stung my eyes and I squeezed Andrés' hand tightly, remembering our story.

When I accepted Christ as my Forgiver and Leader of my life I was a girl, only seven, afraid of being in trouble after stealing bubble gum a year prior. I prayed in my heart and kept my secret. The enemy even shamed me about trusting God, so it was just another thing I buried. But, when I was 23, I felt drawn to God for comfort from deep pain bubbling up from my past.

I had been with Andrés for four years. Our time included a two-month engagement, a quaint New Years' Eve wedding, and two cross-country moves. Our married life was good, but it wasn't easy. At least for me. We fought a lot and I still needed constant assurance of Andrés' love and devotion. To complicate matters, I was afraid to see a therapist for help with my emotions. *What if I am crazy? What if Andrés realizes I really am not loveable?* I felt burdened by our disastrous finances, graduate school demands, and our newly adopted mischievous black lab, Guinness. The enemy tried to tear us apart, and in an outburst, I threatened divorce. But God held us closer still.

My heart ached for real change. I came to a crossroads: I could choose to be honest with God about the state of my brokenness and seek his help *or* continue with numbing, running, and medication with my own self-help. Could I really believe God's word as truth and walk with him to meet my emotional needs? Or would I keep trying to control, strive, and seek love apart from him? How long would I keep running from my deepest pain? How long would I expect Andrés to be everything for me?

I needed Jesus' love. I needed him for everyday challenges. He broke through with a song, sung over me, softening my heart as I peered out the train window at maple trees. He loves *me*, like actually, intensely. I had falsely believed he had been aloof, unconcerned about my suffering, just waiting to bring me to heaven. No wonder I had run so far believing such heresy. I thought he could be my last chance option, like fire insurance, just before I died. As if I could live a full, fun life apart from his control and judgment.

But, sweet friend, he loved me so. He loves me still. He loved me, and by his loving-kindness drew me into his healing arms.

God patiently walked with me another few years, leading me to Poland in 2016. From 23 to 27, I prayed, fell in love reading the Bible, listening to Christian music stations like K-LOVE, and shared my faith with Andrés. At 27 I was baptized by my childhood pastor. My Father lovingly removed things in my life that did not align with his character, reining my heart to align with his. He didn't overwhelm me with guilt, instead, he gave me glimpses of who he was. In return, I was beginning to see who I was, rewriting old records of shame and rejection. Andrés could sense it too, seeing the fruits of love, peace, and self-control springing up in me.

In the stillness of Poland, God invited me to grow once more: could I be content and fulfilled in him, apart from any other relationship? Could I find joy in being alone? Could I love my own company?

Three-thousand miles away in a foreign country was the perfect place for the Lord to challenge my belief. An ocean literally separated me from Andrés! We connected throughout the day, but I still ached with loneliness. I felt exposed, weak, and unseen in an unfamiliar land. Back home I'd get upset when we were apart for a few days, and this assignment was for several months.

I struggled to believe I could be complete without some relationship or accolade to define me. I didn't like being alone. I only felt good when I was checking things off my list—for myself, for others, just constantly doing. *Sit alone and be with my thoughts?* Yikes. *What would I say?*

Life at home was predictable, but it was frequently not purposeful, joyful, or abundant. Living each day believing I was not worthy of true love was exhausting and kept me striving. I was anxious, stressed, and overwhelmed. My heart ached for more, but I couldn't grasp it. I wanted a happy life and to please God, but I couldn't hear him. I thought maybe when I "arrived" at the next good thing I'd find it. I didn't know his heart for me was one of love. I thought I would be loved by doing. And doing things according to my plan, not his.

But God, in his perfect timing, introduced me to the story of Gideon only a month before my Poland departure with a Priscilla Shirer study.[2] The story goes that the Israelites were partially living in the Promised Land. However, they had aggressive idol-worshiping neighbors, the Midianites, who wreaked havoc on them. Then Gideon enters the scene, hiding with his food in a big barrel, afraid of the Midianites when the angel of the Lord appears and says:

> *"The LORD is with you, mighty warrior...Go in the strength you have and save Israel out of Midian's hand. Am I not sending you?"* Judges 6:12b, 14

Gideon doubts God's plan for Gideon to free the Israelites. He even asks for multiple confirmations before he acts on his calling.

> *"Pardon me, my lord," Gideon replied, "but how can I save Israel? My clan is the weakest in Manasseh, and I am the least in my family."* Judges 6:15

You've got to be kidding me! I argued with God. *How could I, in my limited experience and skills, accomplish his calling for me in Poland? Don't you know who I am and what I've done? I'm hopeless! I'll always be broken.* I was unsure what my calling in Poland truly was, outside of completing my professional work, making tons of money to pay off our debt, and maybe being adopted by a nice Polish family to share meals and use their washing machine. Who was I to believe God had dreams for me? What if I was disappointed?

Stricken with loneliness, especially during my first six weeks in Słupsk, God led me to a humble place of surrender. I could either trust him to come alongside me to battle my loneliness and limitations or try the same old junk of performing for praise and defining my worth by other's approval. I had to get my eyes off my fears and insecurities and turn to God, with his infinite wisdom and assuring love. And for goodness sake, if he called me, then he knew I could do with his help!

Praise God, who is so faithful.

Trust in the Lord with all your heart and lean not on your own understanding; in all your ways submit to him, and he will make your paths straight.
Proverbs 3:5-6

I journaled a proclamation weeks after my arrival. "Lord, you are going to sustain me. Sundays I am going to dedicate to you. I will stream podcasts, journal, pray, praise, and pray some more. I will reflect on your goodness and love. You are my comfort. You see me. You are my strength..." God was tearing down one of the biggest lies I had believed, "you are alone and unloved." I became increasingly aware of God's presence surrounding me and his profound, ceaseless love for me. His love was propelling me forward to have hope in him for my future. As someone who has battled depression since childhood, rising hope was a radically new experience. Wow—God loved *me* and had good plans for my life!

As I grew in his love, I began to trust he was working in my life. He had taken away the comforts of home. I felt the only thing I could do was accept his love and plan for me, and trust he was holding the details. He knew the full course of my life, and I began to believe his path was the only one I wanted to follow.

Sweet Sarah, you've run so far. But now it's time to return to my love. Release those lies, and striving, and fears to me. I want to show you my goodness. I want you to know my love. My Father called to my heart.

In the peace of a warm spring evening, I finished my Bible study of Gideon along the babbling brook. I wrote myself a note on the inside flap, recalling my heart's journey where the Lord brought me from February to May of 2016:

I started this study in Quito, Ecuador, then Playas and Guayaquil [Ecuador], then Massachusetts to Slupsk, Poland.

The Lord has great plans for me and my marriage plans to prosper me and not to harm me, plans to give me hope and a future. This study has traveled with me during some challenging weeks emotionally, relationally with Andrés, and spiritually. Gideon was not perfect, but God used him to do great things. I too, will, and am being used for great things. Let my heart stay in alignment with the Lord's plan for my life.

I am not alone here, and I don't have to do it in my own strength. Actually, I'm not meant to! He is working through me day by day in this wonder-

ful place. Lord help me to keep putting one foot in front of the other—let your Word be a lamp to my feet, a light to my path in this season, and for all those yet to come.

In Jesus' name,
Amen

My tiny signature graced the page; a promise between me and my Father.

If not for the painful work in my heart, my pride would have crept in—another type of lie that chokes the joyful, peaceful life Jesus offers. In the past, on the other side of my trials, I had too often believed I succeeded by myself. I was sufficient on my own. Sure, I had to hold on with a white-knuckle grip and fight off mental and physical exhaustion, but I made it. I did it. Or so I thought.

But he gives us more grace. That is why Scripture says: 'God opposes the proud but shows favor to the humble.' Submit yourselves, then, to God. Resist the devil, and he will flee from you. Come near to God and he will come near to you. Wash your hands, you sinners, and purify your hearts, you double-minded.
James 4:6-8

I was horribly sick for a week in high school. Nothing seemed to help. By that Friday, I was napping under my desk in Mrs. P's English class instead of reading The Great

Gatsby. That evening at home, my brother poked me in the stomach, "Does this hurt?" I reeled. A few hours later, a surgeon removed my inflamed appendix. Although I still had to recover from major surgery, I was protected from it rupturing and toxins poisoning my body. God did not leave me in my suffering then, and he did not let me continue to inflict mental pain upon myself when I was in Poland. He drew out the poisonous lies I told myself to heal my heart.

I wasn't meant to strive and earn praise from others. I did not need love from people to feel loved. I did not need to make up for the sins of my past. He was waiting for me to turn from my unstable ways, once anchored on shifting sands. He was with me in the striving, just waiting for me to call out and lead me into his spacious place.[3] He knew me all along and was singing over me with joy.[4] And most of all, I didn't need to earn my Father's love. Despite what my past told me, I couldn't work harder to receive more love, and my mistakes wouldn't remove any love. I was just wildly loved.

My mind was being freed from burdens of anxieties and insecurities, I began believing and seeing the identity he gave me; regardless of what any person, petal, or enemy lie said. His truth kept popping up, confirming his love for me. He spoke to me with words from a podcast, from Bible studies, and from Zig Ziglar's positive Self-Talk cards. I recited these truths over my life each morning - looking at myself in the eye, and I began:

"I, [Sarah], am a [beautiful daughter] of the King, in the will of God, and can do anything through Christ who gives me the strength. I claim the following attributes because I have the mind of Christ, am a confidant of God, and although I am weak in many of these qualities I am specifically told to 'let the weak say I am strong.' By claiming, developing, and using these Biblical qualities, I will become the person God created me to be and will glorify God and benefit mankind."[5]

The Holy Spirit stirred my heart; I began to realize I needed to humbly ask him to help me through my trials and loneliness. Covered by his love was the best place for me. He was inviting me to throw down all my burdens and let him love all of me.

"Faith or fear?" I pondered on a park bench in Słupsk one cloudy Sunday afternoon.

What do I choose? They cannot co-exist. I often give way to anxiety, worry, fear: stomach troubles, racing heart, the tension in my soul, and clenched teeth as I sleep. They all point to a lack of trust in the Lord's promises for me and the work he's doing in my life. Lord, show me how to increase my trust, or have the right kind of trust—mustard seed quality—that blossoms into a great tree with deep roots into your character.

As I sit here, in a park under a willow tree slowly showing its new leaves, ravens poke the grass for food. Matthew chapter six comes to mind; these little ones aren't running around in a frantic way searching for provisions. They calmly go about their work, flying away when they are done. I guess they had their fill! Such small birds, but the Lord knows every one of them. He knows me just as well—he knows my needs and my heart. Why do I worry about these things in life? It's hard to break old habits, habits that have been passed down through my family. I come from a long line of expert worriers. I see the Lord giving me peace when I turn to him, but it still isn't a habit.

Like my Bible study of Gideon is showing me— many battles are spiritual. I can't get far in my own strength, thinking pridefully I can handle it. Obviously not well! I need to admit that my brokenness allows Christ's light to shine through my earthly vessel. It brings the Lord more glory when I allow him to work through me! He uses the foolish, weak things of this world to confuse the wise), things (like myself) that don't make sense with human reasoning, but which God's power can overcome!⁶ I want my weaknesses to be used to point others to him! I want to be empowered to share my struggles with others so they can have hope for their own mistakes.

I want a community here. I need to connect with other believers and not do this journey alone. I pray I would let the Holy Spirit lead me to people and conversations that develop into fellowship and discipleship. I'm scared though. I've never been forward about my faith except to other believers, even then I get worried that I'll offend others or lose a friendship. But I know I am here for a purpose!

Lord, let me grow and be like a tree planted by a stream of water, which yields its fruit in season and whose leaf does not wither—whatever they do prospers. I woke up with the imagery of tree roots in my head this morning. It was no coincidence.

"As the Father has loved me, so I have loved you. Now remain in my love." John 15:9

Did I really believe God loves me as much as he loves his perfect son Jesus? I am not sure I will ever fully grasp that truth until I see him face to face, but I am desperately seeking to know it ever-increasingly. One night in Poland, God gave me a dream—one of me growing an unshakable relationship with him. Seeds planted long ago were finally taking root as insecurities were destroyed by his loving presence. My past was no match for his love for me.

Reflecting on those first six weeks in Poland, I proudly began receiving the identity he gave me, like wrapping up in a cozy robe I never wanted to take off. I was able to rest in his love and explore his heart in safety. Then the unexpected happened, I began to embrace my traumatic experiences as part of my story, letting his perfect love silence my shame and fear. It was an unforced rhythm; a new sense of child-like joy and peace flooded into my life from his presence.

I can look back and see my broken, rejected heart as a little girl in the field. But now I see hope. I see he was singing a lullaby over me; *you are my beloved daughter.*

He's been singing the beautiful chorus all along, and he will never stop.

36

April 2016
Redzikowo, Poland

Google Works Better in Texas

CHAPTER 3

Poland's dreary gray coat of spring mirrored my heart as I settled into my new ex-pat life. It pained me to come home to no one, especially at night after I finished working long hours on base. Coworkers met for dinner downstairs at our hotel, the et Cetera. When I joined them, I would gaze at murals and the arched stone and plaster ceiling as conversations usually circled around project schedules, frustration, and complaining about the dank weather. I ached for big things like friendship and community, and small things like a bed with a top sheet and rectangular pillow. I am an introvert, and at the time I felt I had to literally get to know everyone around me. I longed to know a few people really well. The thought of having small talk with strangers, while adjusting to work demands and a new culture, made me want to curl under my comforter to hide.

Slivers of hope broke through. Sometimes the rain would abate, and the sun would peek out its bright rays warming the damp landscape. I was in a new country and curious to explore it, but I wasn't courageous to venture out too much alone. In the evenings I would call Andrés or my good friend Iulia and cry.

I had become friends with Iulia only six months before my Polish assignment. We had both been praying for a godly friend in our lives. In her matter of fact, funny manner, one day she saw my desk had a stone with James 4:8 on it. She interrogated, "Are you a Christian?!" with passion and intensity; we became instant friends. We began going on walks at lunch, cooking together, and meeting up with her vibrant friends on the weekends. She told me stories of growing up in Romania and loving her pet duck. I taught her new exercise routines and how to make chocolate truffles. Her laugh embraced everyone within earshot.

She felt God leading us to pray together for our coworkers and each other before work every day. Iulia, or Iulita (sweet little Iulia as I like to call her), taught me about bold, honest prayers, and showed me more of God's loving character. I was in awe of her and her friends' enthusiasm and vibrancy. She always said, "We love you, God." Inside, I was still a scared, wounded child and didn't know I was fully loved or how to return it. But I knew I felt God's love when I was with Iulia.

All alone in Poland, I resorted to my comfort zone: quietly soak in the surroundings as my extroverted colleagues were abuzz around me. Some Sundays I went to a local coffee shop, Kaffeina, to eat tomato soup with sunflower seeds (zupa pomidorowa). I longed to be part of the community. I'd bring my Bible and journal, hoping some nice local Christian would befriend me and invite me to church.

Iulia practically became my friend like that, so why couldn't it happen again? My other hope was to find a nice Polish family to "adopt me"—have me for meals and let me use their washing machine (instead of the one at work that was constantly busy).

Six weeks in, I still had not seen progress on these dreams. For forty hours a week, I was stuck at work in a cold, damp building with whispers of its dark past—the padded double door into the common workspace, the barred armory room, and the old drafty windows overlooking the airfield. Some said Hitler frequented this site en route to his hideout in Northeast Poland. Heinous plans had been made on this land.

Spring was sleepily arriving one grass shoot at a time as I remembered a word of encouragement from Iulia. Something was about to change.

> *"Do not fear, for I am with you; do not anxiously look about you, for I am your God. I will strengthen you and help you, surely I will uphold you with my righteous right hand."* Isaiah 41:10 NASB

It was a typical Thursday. I was next to the windows with the portable heater cranked, wearing my steel-toe boots, thermals, jeans, and a fleece pullover. Around me, people went about their business. Peter complained, this time about assignment agreement terms, in his German American accent, chewing the corner of his glasses between thoughtful breaths. Katie bounced around, warm and bubbly, as she worked at her makeshift standing desk of legal

boxes. Ismael quietly sent me IM's practicing his Polish—
"DD," which was our chat lingo for "dzien dobre", (good
morning/afternoon). I flipped through site drawings and
silently worried about my own assignment agreement and
tried to appear busy.

What did I get myself into? I sighed quietly. It hadn't
even been two months; many of my coworkers were returning stateside for good this weekend. I would be alone, and
I wasn't going home to visit until July. I needed to learn
to drive these crazy roads, with endless two-lane round-
abouts and "suggested" speed limits in kilometers and the
added challenge of my driving manual in our Skoda Rapid.
(Which I originally thought was a VW *Rabbit* because of the
language barrier at the airport...)

I was disappointed I would lose my meal compan-
ions, especially Jon, who went on daily site walks with me.
The previous day, I even shared part of my testimony with
him—that my trust in Jesus was changing my heart. I had
been anxious, depressed, even suicidal at times, but now was
hopeful, medication-free, and purposeful. I had never told
anyone my testimony so frankly, especially to a coworker
who didn't share the same faith. God was already making me
brave in those short weeks.

The enemy tried to distract me with worry about my
next steps. I needed to move out of my hotel room and into
an apartment upstairs. *At least I could cook for myself and
have a great balcony overlooking the city,* I mused.

Suddenly an email interrupted my train of thought; it
was from my friend, Jazmin, in Houston. The subject line
read: "Church you may want to check out" with just a link:

"http://ccrwz.pl/en."

I had seen her and her new husband, Matt, in Austin for their beautiful ceremony during my first home visit three weeks after I moved to Poland.

I clicked the link and scrolled through photos of joyful people, baptisms, celebrations, and surprisingly their website was in English (thanks to my friend, Gosia). I knew this was my home church. Their next service was that night! But I wanted to scope out the location with a plan to attend Sunday. In the cool of the evening, I strolled down the cobblestones, through the park, and along the river to see where it was for Sunday.

Kościół Rzeki Wody Żywej, translated Rivers of the Living Water Christian Center, 2 Filmowa Street

No car was needed; it was in the heart of Słupsk and only a 20-minute walk from the et Cetera. I had passed the church numerous times on my journeys around town. It didn't seem like I had the right place. The stone building was a residential/commercial for a small blue wall placard with a cross and their name.

Within fifteen minutes of receiving Jazmin's email, I shot off a message to Andrés; I was elated! I also emailed the church:

Hi! I am new in Słupsk and have been searching to find a strong Bible-believing church with some services in English and am encouraged by your website. Is there a service this weekend I can attend? I look forward to hearing from you soon.

In Christ,
Sarah

I clicked send and glanced out the old panes. Suddenly, a magnificent double rainbow lit up the gray airfield. A laugh escaped my lips as tears of joy welled up. Exceedingly good things were coming. "Ok, Lord, you've got me in your hands." This was my new home. My eyes shifted off my circumstances and onto my Father.

During my first Sunday service, I was warmly greeted on the street by Kuba and he directed me through the large oak door into the checkered hall and up four flights of stairs. Justyna's bright blue eyes sparkled as she smiled "Oh, American! Let me find my sister. She'll translate for you…" I thought, *why can't you, miss? Your English is amazing!*

Sweet, petite Gosia; her small stature was no match for her energy and joy. She welcomed me to sit beside her and offered to translate the service word for word. We began with worship, as I attempted to read and sing Polish. Gosia was part of the band - actually, it was comprised of all her siblings and brothers-in-law. People were joyfully clapping, raising hands, and saying "Alleluja!" and "Jezusa!" The warm beige walls paled in comparison to the glow I felt in my heart from God's presence.

Gosia's parents, Marek and Ala, were the lead pastors but were traveling out of town. We live-streamed a partner church's message in Koszalin with Pastor Paweł Godowa. As the sermon started, Gosia returned to my side, leaned toward me, and spoke life to my weary heart. Unfortunately, I can't tell you much about what he said, I didn't take notes. I was awestruck by the power of God's presence over the gathering and how he provided beyond my wildest expectations and prayers. God's goodness amazed me. Of the sermon's message, all I recall is that it was Truth with a capital "T" and life-giving. God placed me here for a *purpose*. It was unlike anything I'd ever heard. God spoke hope directly to my anxious heart.

As I had accepted Jesus as my Savior when I was a girl, I knew I had a tiny spark in me. But that day, May 1, 2016, God leaned in close, and gently breathed on the embers in my heart, setting them ablaze by his Spirit. He was working in me—preparing me for the growth and healing to come. New hope rose within me, his brilliant light cast off the dark cloak of my past burden and shame. I could feel God stepping into my life, embracing me in his arms. "Come, my daughter, I have so much to show you. Let me love you only as I can…"

Little did I know my friend, Ismael, had already found the church. He had been attending for weeks and even crashed their band practices to play the drums. I had just never asked! Silly me, believing I would be the only Jesus-lover on the engineering team.

Ironically, I came to church just two days after he returned home. It did create some confusion when I arrived, but now we all laugh about it. Gosia asked, "So where are you from?" I nervously said, "America. I'm just visiting…" afraid to expose my position at Redzikowo's base. "Wow! We just had another American visit. Do you know Ismael?" "Actually, yes." "Wonderful, welcome, Sarah! You don't have to tell us more about your work," Gosia winked. Laughing awkwardly, I nodded and sighed a wave of relief.

Over the airfield, I looked out to the rainbow and wiped my tears. I replied to Jazmin, *"How did you find this church?!!"* I had searched, posted on chat forums, reached out to missionaries, submitted prayer requests, but no place was the right fit. I had resolved to take a two-hour train ride to Gdansk once a month to have some sort of fellowship with other believers.

Her reply came quickly, short and sweet:

"Lol google :)"

I could see God warmly chuckling over me as he unfolded his provision for my Polish family, my community, and more importantly, the deep work to restore my heart.

April 2016
Czołpino, Poland

Broken Treasures

CHAPTER 4

"These stupid directions!" Jon complained. "Let me see the map," Peter said gruffly. We drove down meandering roads lined with stoic trees and rolling green fields beyond. Siri said, "turn left" then "turn right" and we did. The car slowed to a stop at a dead-end in a desolate field with a babbling brook and light sandy dunes in the distance. I sighed, unbuckling from the back seat, and stepped onto the concrete pavers. *Will we ever see the elusive nature park on the Baltic?* I pondered. The peace of the countryside filled my lungs. I took a few selfies in the glorious sun and crisp breeze, soaking in the beauty as my coworkers conspired on a new route.

Backtracking some kilometers, we found the entrance, "Słowiński Park Narodowy" (Slowinski National Park) with a small parking area surrounded by evergreens. A constant whir surrounded us like a noisy freeway.

A path of pavers and a wooden fence led us through a stubby pine forest. The trees seemed perfectly spaced, and a soft bed of moss covered the earth. It was unlike anything I had ever seen. Most trees had large kinks in their trunks, yet the upper portions managed to right themselves. What had caused them to have such a bent?

White dunes rose before us in a clearing. The whir grew in intensity. I tucked my scarf closer to my neck and took off to the water's break line. The sea called, despite the nippy air, I slipped off my sneakers. Snap! Photos memorialized my delight with my toes in the surf.

Waves! Big waves crashed into the smooth white shore. The tiny sand particles squeaked as I strolled and searched for my delight: sea glass. Actual sea glass!

I looked up at the dunes that gave way to the sand and then the vast sea stretching out to the horizon. No boats, houses, developments, shops, or man-made anything was in sight. Pure, unblemished Baltic beaches welcomed me. I ditched my coworkers and ventured alone, breathing in the sweet sea air.

"A perfect sea treasure!" I rejoiced. The glass was tumbled completely and vibrant green. I was home. Smooth pebble patches of reds, greens, oranges, and whites popped up along the beach. I gravitated toward them seeking out more glass; they did not disappoint. The pockets of my jeans bulged with smooth stones and sea glass after an hour had passed.

Rounded on all edges, the soft, thick frosted glass, caught the sunlight and was set aglow among the rocks and sand. A beacon of light calling out to be picked up and treasured.

Proud of my riches, I arranged them on my nightstand that evening, taking photos to complete my Instagram collage of the adventure. "Polish treasures," I captioned it. Each piece was delightful in appearance and touch. They were unlike anything I had ever seen.

You may be wondering why, as my dear Andrés, broken pieces of glass bottles could be anything apart from litter, yet I challenge you to consider how sea glass is made. How many years of tumbling in the surf does it take to produce a smooth piece? Decades, even half a century is needed for perfectly frosted gems.

Since my time in Poland, God has brought me through my own tumbling process. I spent much of my life believing I was one of those broken vessels, a disposed glass shard, shipwrecked, and abandoned. But God, in his mercy and beautiful redemption, didn't let my story end there. Instead of garbage, he spoke love, *you are a unique treasure, set apart, designed to receive and reflect my light. That's the beauty of my design.*

Growing up I felt a pull in my heart for deep connection but was left unsatisfied, except for moments in nature, where my soul found rest. I knew I wanted joy, but childhood innocence was stolen from me; how could I delight in the small things? Who could love me, a broken child covered in shame? I tried to be a careful, good-natured girl, but I didn't know how to have a relationship with the Lord. I didn't know any better. I was stuck riding unstable waves of my emotions. I acted how I thought I needed to for others to like me, or at least like the "good" me. My soul churned in agony. I hated myself.

As a preteen, I tried Bible studies, but I felt disconnected from God and I didn't hear an audible voice, so I didn't think he spoke to me. My mind was cluttered with pain from my trauma and depression, but I couldn't process them alone. I didn't even know I was experiencing those things, so the feeling that registered was deep shame. The Bible and worship music fell flat. I was part of the youth group and had a few sweet moments with the Lord at Christian camps, but it all fell apart going back into my normal home environment. It was more about doing the right thing than believing God wanted to reveal himself to me, let alone heal me, or truly believe he adored me! I was a young girl, carrying adult-sized burdens. I thought family members loved me out of obligation. Why wouldn't God be the same way?

I didn't trust people enough to open up. I couldn't even articulate my deepest regrets or feelings on paper lest a sibling finds my journal and expose me. Nor did I really believe my life was atypical, I thought I had to cope and get over it. I thought everyone was carrying shame and pain and bearing it alone.

I was agreeable, kind, and hardworking, but inside I was tormented. I had an existential crisis as a child! What was the purpose of life? Why was I even born? Why would I want to have my own children one day if they would suffer the same fate? Why would I want to live forever? I always saw myself alone in heaven, going on and on, forever forgotten. It paralyzed me with fear and can still try to grip my heart today. I felt unseen and unworthy. Dirty. I preferred everything to just go dark, like before my first memory. Then I would never have to be or feel ever again. That was how depression stole any hope for my future.

God spoke hope into my life in Poland; *My daughter, I can take what's broken and rough and make it smooth. You are not too broken for me.* As he promises in the book of Isaiah:

> *"I will lead the blind by ways they have not known, along unfamiliar paths I will guide them; I will turn the darkness into light before them and make the rough places smooth. These are the things I will do; I will not forsake them."* Isaiah 42:16

I began to believe and feel God's heart for me. I was never forsaken. He always had hope for me and my story. He was leading me out of the brokenness of depression onto a new path in Poland. I had seen much of my life as garbage, full of lies and shame of what I'd done and what had been done to me. My heart was sick from the constant pounding of lies. I struggled, relying only on my strength to overcome. *You're a failure. You hurt people. You're an abuser. You're worthless. You're unloved.* The enemy made his own violent waves—ones to harm and drown my hope. He had been effective for so long, but then the tides turned.

Jesus stepped in, arms wide, calling my name.

Sarah!

I let go and ran to him.

I desperately needed to surrender and let him wash over my life and bring healing with his gentle, unconditional love. I couldn't smooth out my brokenness alone. I needed Jesus.

He met me and smoothed my raw heart as I released my memories to him, walking on the beach. A new journey of healing began. I had been too blinded by my painful past to see that his goodness and love were accessible to me. Unlike what I had believed, I didn't have to clean up to be loved.

49

Embarking on an unfamiliar path in a foreign land, I welcomed his warmth. Uninhibited by fear of others, I finally felt free to be me. I felt free to be loved. Jesus led me with love and taught me to delight in him as I walked the Baltic shores.

Throughout my time in Poland, I returned to the Baltic on countless occasions. I loved windy days, the surf was large, and the pebbles and sea glass were plentiful.

One cool, sunny Saturday in late April, I gave myself a pep talk to drive out to Słowiński Park. The same park my coworkers couldn't even find with maps and a GPS. It would be at least 45 minutes of driving down curvy roads. If I made a wrong turn, my GPS would be useless since I didn't have cell service to correct the course. It also meant I had to navigate back by memory.

I finished my fried eggs, salad, melon, and lots of coffee. As I was leaving the breakfast nook, Ismael appeared, looking cozy in a black hoodie, "What are you up to today?" I asked. Our other coworkers had gone to Denmark for a long weekend. He shrugged, "Nothing really." On a whim, I asked him to join me.

We drove those narrow roads together; he encouraged me as it was my first time driving out of town. Like a sweet granny, I preferred a steady 60 km/hour pace. My brain was wired for mph; my nerves went haywire going "80" down a country road! Ismael and I laughed, and he told me, "You're doing great!" As cars rapidly approached, I gave-way, partially pulling off the road, and they zoomed past. Then I continued with my tortoise-paced journey to the sea.

I had planned to listen to podcasts and praise music on my drive to calm me, but since Ismael joined, I didn't want to impose. Honestly, I was afraid he would dislike it and reject me. Then I'd really be all alone in a foreign country.

Without delays or wrong turns, we arrived at our destination. The cobalt sea and soft, pale sands emerged through the bent pine forest. April definitely was not beach season, and the wind bit at us sharply and often.

Ismael and I wandered the pristine beach at our own speeds and paths. I strolled and prayed, comforted by the repetition of wave crashing after wave. I sifted through the rock piles in search of sea glass. My mind would drift, I'd start to pray, then get distracted looking for glass. I was completely in the moment—not planning tomorrow or even the rest of the day. My worries drowned in the roar of the sea.

I must have walked several kilometers, as I looked down to full pockets of treasure. My companion was out of sight.

I paused. In the undisturbed sand, I sprawled out my body, my arms, and legs squeaking in grains. *A sand angel!* I giggled. I felt God's presence all around me.

Eventually, I found Ismael again. I climbed up a dune to overlook the sea. Two people emerged from a wooded path beyond, and they offered to take my photo. Did I speak Polish to them? Perhaps. The wind blew my hair as a genuine grin spread across my face. Ismael, the size of an ant, standing below on the beach was captured in the shot.

The first time I met my Polish friend Beata, she told me she saw this photo on Facebook and said, "I could see Jesus looking out through your eyes." No one had ever personified his life in me in such a beautiful way.

Despite my best efforts, my healing process could not be accelerated. My heart, like sea glass, couldn't be made beautiful overnight. It took time for the Lord to work in my mind and relieve pain from trauma. I had hidden in my shame for more than two decades. I know he can provide immediate release and healing, but for me, I needed his deep, slow work to smooth the rough gouges of my heart. I also couldn't submit to his work until I knew his tender heart for me. Could I trust this new pain was actually bringing healing? Did I believe he was in control and wanted what was best for me? Was he really a good Father and loved me unconditionally? A wave of his love swept over me. I was starting to see the good from the hard work of being washed from my past sin and shame.

I came up for air.

I could breathe without the weight of shame. I enjoyed daily activities without being bombarded by critical, hopeless thoughts.

Removing lies one by one, I finally was able to process my darkest times, but no longer relive them. Instead, I looked at myself—hurt, and lost, and had compassion. I reached out in my mind, scoop myself up, weeping for poor, broken Sarah. "You are seen and loved, little one. There is good to come! Just hang on. God has great things for you." As I smoothed her thick hair, pulling her close to my chest.

My hopes rose as the Lord bandaged my wounds. The process kept me running to him, resting under the shadow of his wings. I was rough and exposed and needed the reassurance of his love. I had been broken apart—so he could build me back up—anchored on the rock of his love.

"I am the Lord your God, who teaches you what is best for you, who directs you in the way you should

go. If only you had paid attention to my commands, your peace would have been like a river, your well-being like the waves of the sea." Isaiah 48:18

Remembering my times on the Baltic, the Lord gave me healing, wave after wave; I was done rejecting his love and truth. His peace saturated my mind. It was easy to agree to his good plans for my life—as I focused on his love—and trusted he knew me through and through. He knew where I had been, and where I was going. I let go of the broken shards of glass in my clenched fists. My wounds were raw and infected. I was safest when I fell apart in Jesus' love and healing hand. It was counter-intuitive, but by his grace, I started to feel the sweet freedom on the other side of surrender.

Healing brings beauty from pain. The broken glass in the waves is not forsaken or discarded, but revitalized as it is washed, tumbled, and washed again. Looking back, I had a choice to embrace: As a follower of Jesus, I am not defined by how broken I was, but by his identity shining through me. I relaxed in his waves, allowing them to smooth my sharp edges. I was transforming more into his likeness and beauty, from this place my truest self emerged. His work in my heart began to shine through the pieces of my heart. I know there is hope for your own painful story; Jesus can redeem the worst life has thrown at you too.

I was broken. Christ met me there. He ran to me; despite all the times I ran from him. From my broken state, I felt how he carefully handles a delicate, unloved heart. I have been healed because he loves me too much to leave me drowning in lies, gasping for life, for purpose, for love.

He gathers the lambs and carries them in the fold of his garment. Isaiah 40:11 CSB

Friend, I was healed to share this hope with you. What is clenched in your fists? What is it costing you? Let his love wash over you. Release the shame, the lies, the fears into the surf.

> *"Here I am! I stand at the door and knock. If anyone hears my voice and opens the door, I will come in and eat with that person, and they with me."*
> Revelation 3:20

Jesus opens his arms and offers comfort, a safe hideaway from our suffering. He is not ashamed or surprised by our broken hearts. Don't send him away like an unexpected houseguest. Instead, try inviting him in and allowing him to help you tidy up your life. He went to the cross for *all* of it.

Let Jesus in, friend. Let him bring beauty from your brokenness. Journal it. Tell a trusted friend or counselor. Bring the dark things to light so they don't hold power over you anymore. Jesus knows. He is pursuing our hearts—as the apostle, Paul wrote:

> *But God demonstrates his own love for us in this: While we were still sinners, Christ died for us.*
> Romans 5:8

The price Jesus paid on the cross is enough to overcome the darkest parts of our stories. You don't need to clean up to receive his love, no, sweet friend. He's the healer, the captive-freer, the lover of our souls. He has already overcome, bearing the cost of our sins, once and for all. Step into his love, friend. Let your story shine as his light radiates through your beautifully broken places.

This is the message we have heard from him and declare to you: God is light; in him, there is no darkness at all. If we claim to have fellowship with him and yet walk in the darkness, we lie and do not live out the truth. But if we walk in the light, as he is in the light, we have fellowship with one another, and the blood of Jesus, his Son, purifies us from all sin.
1 John 1:5-7

I will never stop singing God's praise for the goodness of his restoration over my broken life. But I'm not done healing. I need to surrender *daily*. I need to constantly invite Jesus to refresh me and help me walk in the Truth: I am beautiful, loved, and forgiven. I have survived many waves of life, but now I know I am being restored and washed by Jesus' constant love.

My green "gem" among the pebbles and surf.

Winds of change were coming as Jesus stirred
my heart to rest in his quiet, secure love for me.
My friend Ismael, photobombing below, as he
encouraged me to explore from the beach.

My Polish paradise—a beautiful, empty beach for miles.

Sweet Grace

CHAPTER 5

On one rainy evening, I walked home from my friend Katie's house, my pink and white umbrella bobbing through the forest. Birds sang from their perches, but every other person in Słupsk seemed to be cozy at home. I loved being alone on a little caper. The rhythmic pitter-patter of the droplets on the tree's leaves fell down onto my umbrella; I smiled at the sound. Troubles with delayed reviews at work, tense conversations with contractors, and my own critical voice melted away on my walk, and many walks thereafter. Grace came with every persistent drop. I let the Lord wash away the tension as I prayed. I trusted him with my heart, and I was learning to walk in his daily grace.

With each day I felt I could stand unashamed before Jesus, and increasingly so, in front of others. I am in awe of where I was, hardly compared to where I am now: hope-filled and forgiven *because* of Jesus' work on the cross. I learned I could give the sweet gift of grace to friends, coworkers, and my family after I received it myself. Each walk and each decision to trust in God's goodness and affection toward me made each day easier, as I grew to learn how life should be lived.

But he said to me, "My grace is sufficient for you, for my power is made perfect in weakness." Therefore I will boast all the more gladly about my weaknesses, so that Christ's power may rest on me. 2 Corinthians 12:9

My shortcomings only remind me of the daily need to be dependent on his grace to strengthen me. His grace was freely given when I reached out and asked in faith with prayer. I continue to soak in the deep peace from his presence, trusting his grace will always be enough.

On the last and greatest day of the festival, Jesus stood and said in a loud voice, "Let anyone who is thirsty come to me and drink. Whoever believes in me, as Scripture has said, rivers of living water will flow from within them."
John 7:38

The old hymn "Come Thou Fount of Blessing" speaks of souls 'prone to wander' from his love, and I find it to be true of my experience. My weary soul was prone to wander from his love and strive in the flesh as if that were my destiny. I got caught up in daily trials, searching for self-worth in performance. As I poured into others, I thought I'd find fulfillment as they poured back into me. But I didn't ask God to fill me with his love. I didn't believe he wanted to satisfy the deepest yearnings of my soul. Nothing seemed to quench my thirst because deep down, I didn't believe his love and grace were for me. I had been emptying myself for others in my own strength. I wasn't receiving Jesus' boundless grace for the day and it was a worn-out life. As I began to walk in grace, Jesus shut down the enemy's broken record that I had too long accepted as truth— I was hopeless and unlovable. Now I can see that the Holy Spirit was waiting for me to understand how truly miserable life can be without his grace, without love, without understanding the only good life is a life with Christ, in rest and trust.

Sweet Grace.

Jesus brought me to his ceaseless springs. Falling down and unashamed, I drank from his streams of his grace. My heart heard his voice. *You are worth it. You are mine; you are precious and honored in my sight.*

Before Poland, I struggled with knowing what grace meant to me. I hadn't experienced it. How could I receive grace? My harsh inner judge screamed, "You're dirty and unworthy." I couldn't tell others about my darkest thoughts and sins; how could I invite Jesus into my brokenness? In my own strength, I couldn't find a way out of my mental mess. My past had ruined me and gave me an outlook of distrust and negativity. I couldn't see Jesus in those moments. I did not yet believe in a loving God who would have compassion for me because all I heard was that I deserved my pit of darkness. I had horrible, shameful sins. Where was grace for that? I needed the real, raw gospel, at its fullest power to free me from the self-condemnation of sin. I didn't know how to find it. As a girl, Sunday school songs meant to encourage my budding faith did the opposite. "Let my light shine?" I didn't know how to shine. Who would love such a sinful girl? How could I share Jesus' love when I didn't believe in it myself?

God kept seeking me and teaching me about his grace in Poland.

Sarah, come into my grace. I am covering you. You are safe with me, come out of the storm.

SWEET GRACE

For all have sinned and fallen short of the glory of God. Romans 3:23

Christians talk about preaching the gospel and how it changes lives. The phrase may be foreign to you or so wrapped up in cultural noise and weaponized that it's even become something you avoid knowing more about. I remember feeling burdened and guilty for not sharing my faith as a child. 'Gospel' in its original Greek, euangelion, means "good news."[7] This language was borrowed and repurposed from imperial Rome; each time Caesar conquered new lands (pillaging, kidnapping, conquering) this was termed 'euangelion'.[8] Christ-followers at that time knew people needed directions to the one true God. God who loved, who saved, who wanted his love and goodness to flow through all people, sharing and giving all that they had to one another. Those followers knew Christ as king, not Caesar. At its core, the story of Jesus is meant to be good news to the weary, broken, marginalized, and lost. In his famous sermon on the mount, Jesus said, those who mourn, who thirst, who strive for true peace, who are poor in spirit—these are the people of God's kingdom, and for whom he has come.[9] In modern times some have distorted the hope of the good news by emphasizing works-based, self-effort, and guilt-laden rule-following will make God approve of you. But that is not the true gospel. This false narrative of the gospel was one I had readily believed until I experienced the freedom of God's grace poured out on my story in Poland.

The gospel at its core is a beautiful love letter from our Creator to us. The Lord created a perfect world in love. He is the great artist, creator, author, from beginning to end.

We were formed in his heart, purposed, and born into God's delight, into flourishing. But our first parents were deceived into thinking God was holding his best from them. A small seed of doubt was sewn, and it grew into actions that separated us from this closeness with God. Humans forever after have faced both literal and spiritual death, destruction, war, sin. You feel it in your bones, don't you, friend? A yearning for wholeness and union: with God, with others, with nature, and within our own minds and bodies.

But though God's heart was grieved, a plan was set, a shift in the cosmos through Christ's sacrifice, for all humanity. Jesus' love for us was greater than death and now we live in this "upside-down kingdom," where the first are last and the last are first .[10,11] When we know God we know ourselves. When we walk faithfully in our belovedness, into freedom through Jesus, who indwells within our physical bodies through his resurrection. God's heart is for this life to be shared. This life is expansive—it welcomes the betrayed, it has room for the sick, the lost, those whom society would prefer to remain hidden. Jesus proclaimed the good news in a synagogue that he came to bind up the brokenhearted, free captives, and give sight to the blind. [12] He came as a gentle healer to restore us and fulfill all the promises written about him. One of Jesus' names in the Old Testament is Immanuel—meaning 'God with us'— God's heart never was to forsake us in our brokenness but to bring us back to our first love.[13]

For God so loved the world that he gave his one and only Son, that whoever believes in him shall not perish but have eternal life. John 3:16

I believe Jesus is God, and that they also love each other, with the Holy Spirit, in a mysterious Trinity of life-giving love and connection. Like how people have mind, body, and spirit, God has three unique facets and humanity is being invited deeper and deeper into this sacred union to know his heart. It seems crazy—how could a perfect God send the Son he loves to die for imperfect people? Because he first loved us. God's sweet grace is a gift we didn't deserve. This gift invites us into a close relationship with Jesus, the Father, and his Spirit, when we turn to him, acknowledge our broken state, and receive Jesus as our forgiver and leader.

As far as the east is from the west, so far has he removed our transgressions from us. As a father has compassion on his children, so the Lord has compassion on those who fear him. Psalm 103:12-13

The simplest way I can tell you the good news is this— you don't have to measure up. Jesus did for you and loves you and wants to have a relationship with you. He wants to speak to your heart right now. He knows everything you were, are, and will be and has good purposes for your life. He's wild about you. He's always been.

"And when he finds [the sheep], he joyfully puts it on his shoulders and goes home. Then he calls his friends and neighbors together and says, 'Rejoice with me; I have found my lost sheep.'" Luke 15:5-6

In Poland, Jesus lifted me up and rejoiced. I was found, his lamb held close to his heart. Could I accept a gift I didn't deserve? Could I let my good Shepherd bring me back into his grace? In turn, could I offer grace to myself to be freed from shame?

I found freedom from myself when I let go of self-condemnation and believed I was truly forgiven and loved as God's daughter.

I wasn't enough.

I'll never be enough.

But Jesus is.

He stepped in to fill the gaping hole. I could stop striving and receive, drinking deeply of his grace. Friend, deep healing was on its way.

Let us approach God's throne of grace with confidence, so that we may receive mercy and find grace to help us in your time of need. Hebrews 4:16

May 2016
Słupsk, Poland

Testimony Sunday

CHAPTER 6

"Sarah, would you like to share your testimony at next Sunday's meeting?" Gosia translated in her polished British-English accent for her father, Marek. We strolled along the Baltic, teal-blue waves gently lapping the shore. I had only gone to the church, Rivers of the Living Waters Christian Centre, for two weeks, and the Siudek family welcomed me as their own, inviting me to several meals and even a birthday celebration.

I responded warmly to Gosia and Marek I would, though I had a pit in my stomach. I had never shared publicly about my dark past of abuse. The Spirit spoke through Gosia as fear and shame flooded my mind, "Power comes from sharing our testimonies together," Gosia encouraged.

The Thursday before my testimony I felt a breakthrough approach. I wrote a reflection and prayer.

*The Lord can take me out of my pit of depression,
my pit of shame, and anger. Last night I prayed
for the Lord to remove the pain and shame of
my past abuse. I felt something leave my body
and I became lighter. A weight was lifted. I have
forgiven others and I am forgiven! I cannot keep
holding on to the pain. I am changed by my past,
but I am not going to be imprisoned by it any
longer.*

Surrounded by dignitaries and servicemen and women, I
stood in a fancy tent eating hors d'oeuvres for the ceremonious groundbreaking of the military base. I borrowed
Gosia's cream suit jacket and wore a raspberry hand-me-
down blouse from Iulia. I felt lost among the sea of dress
uniforms. Apprehensively, I scanned tables lined with mul-
titudes of pickled fish and mysterious offerings but found
a fondue table with fruit and pastries. As an anxious eater
in socially awkward situations, I dove into the sweets. Mid-
bite, Roy approached me, "So I heard you found a church?"
He said in his warm, southern drawl. I half-choked and
stood like a deer in headlights; I had been noticed! My mind
reeled, *back home, us New Englanders keep faith to ourselves,
especially at work!* I reasoned with myself. *Who is this guy?*
God nudged me, "It's ok. Say yes!" I let out an awkward
laugh and invited Roy to church with me. I would now have
to share my testimony with a colleague.

On Sunday, Roy and I carpooled. He was a kind, bubbly father-figure and made me feel at ease. The church
warmly welcomed us. Gosia was beaming to translate for
another person! And I did not die of embarrassment having

a coworker join me at church. Actually, I appreciated Roy's assuring company.

We sang Psalm 40 as tears swept over me. The Lord knew it was my melody.

I waited patiently for the Lord;
He turned to me and heard my cry.
He lifted me out of the slimy pit,
Out of the mud and mire;
He set my feet on a rock
And gave me a firm place to stand.
He put a new song in my mouth,
A hymn of praise to our God.
Many will see and fear the Lord
And put their trust in him.
Psalm 40:1-3

Before Poland, I never related to that Psalm. I had never felt free. Stuck in a pit? Absolutely. Covered in the mud of my mistakes? Definitely. I'd sling it at myself and help the enemy with a shovel. But finding true high ground with a song of praise, unashamed? Sweet friend, the Lord gave me such powerful encouragement!

Psalm 40 was my story. God saw me in the pit. He gave me a new song of hope while he bent down to rescue me in his perfect timing.

After worshiping, I stood with conviction and declared God's faithfulness over my life to a room full of mostly strangers. Gosia translated every word, despite my interrupting stream of tears. The church body leaned in, and I felt loved and known as the Holy Spirit was moving through us. And most surprisingly, I did not feel shame. I felt empowered! Hope awoke deep within my soul; hope I had never known.

Consequently, faith comes from hearing the message, and the message is heard through the word about Christ. Romans 10:17

Our faith grows as we hear God's truth and let it soak into our minds. It was finally time for me to hear my own voice declare God's faithfulness over my story. Something deep in my soul was solidified as God mended and strengthened me to let my song ring out.

Here's my testimony as written in my teal journal dated May 15, 2016:

This opportunity to give my testimony today couldn't have been more perfect timing but leading up to today I was dreading it. I thought I'd have a peaceful Saturday writing and reflecting, but instead, I was depressed, homesick, and discouraged. This morning I realized giving my testimony would be the exact thing I needed to remember and share all the wonderful things, loving things the Lord has done in my life. In my head, I know the Lord is who he is, yesterday, today, and forever, but my feelings are fickle, and I forget often. The enemy loves to steal my hope and trust in God. But today I am here to proclaim what he has freed and is freeing me from while renewing my hope.

I grew up going to a non-denominational church and accepted Christ into my heart when I was seven. But I was living in an unhealthy family—my dad was unfaithful and there was lots of tension. There were also inappropriate relationships with my siblings and abuse. I was in the middle of it. I rejected the Lord's love and goodness for about 15 years. I couldn't see him as a Father. He never left me; despite my wandering now I see how he continued to bless me and protect me.

He saved me from hurting myself despite my rampant depression. He even blessed me with my husband, now married for five years. The stress of life, grad school, marriage, depression, and finances all came to a head four years ago. I had a choice—I could keep medicating my depression with pills and keep my ugly, impatient, controlling, harsh heart or I could invite the Lord to help me.

It has been a slow process, but I can see God's persistence not to let me wander. He is so merciful and has helped heal wounds of my past, I have forgiven and asked for forgiveness. As the Lord has renewed my mind, taking away shame and insecurity, I hear the humble nudge of the Holy Spirit more often.

One nudge led me to seek wisdom in tithing. My husband, Andrés, did not understand my desire to tithe and thought God was rich enough and had some distrust of the Church. But we found an amazing biblical financial class and he was willing to take it. We were given hope and a plan *for our finances. The class changed our hearts to see all we have is a gift from God. He has charged us to be wise stewards of it. Our first step for this process is paying off all our debts - in March of last year, we owed $256,000 (about 1 mil. PLN) in cars, credit cards, but mostly student loans. We promised each other to work as a team and pay it off in four more years. Through this past year we have already paid off $60,000 and we aim to pay off $80,000 in 2016. Every month we do our budget, God pours in more than we planned in the form of financial blessings, gifts, and meals from friends.*

We are finally becoming a unified team. God is changing my husband's heart—he now even encourages me with scripture. It's extremely difficult to be away from him, but I know God is changing my heart here. He is showing me his love is enough, he is truly with me even when I feel completely alone. He took me out of the comforts of my family and routine at home and is testing and growing my trust and love in him. I want him to heal me from depression for good and I know he is able! I am taking it one day at a time.

I desire to do your will, my God;
your law is within my heart.
I proclaim your saving acts in the great assembly,
I do not seal my lips, Lord,
as you know.

I do not hide your righteousness in my heart;
I speak of your faithfulness and your saving help.
I do not conceal your love and your faithfulness
from the great assembly.
Psalm 40:8-10

Bravely I sang the story of my life to the Church of the Rivers of the Living Water. Jesus came to save the broken, hurting, messy parts of me. He came to reclaim what sin had stolen. He wasn't ashamed or surprised by the ugliness of my sin—but he gave me the choice to continue in my pain. Jesus patiently waited for me to recognize the ache in my soul could only be satisfied by his love. I finally had enough! My soul was ready for change as sunshine streamed through the windows of the church's sanctuary on Filmowa Street. I was running to Jesus and throwing off my burdens.

For too long I had bottled up the pain and shame. I also suffered emotionally as I recalled my past, reliving it again and again, triggered by different movies, TV, books, or conversations—all typical symptoms of post-traumatic stress disorder .[14] In college, I finally saw a therapist. I was diagnosed with major depression and PTSD and they recommended antidepressants. I was reluctant to try medication, I believed I needed to deal with the pain myself and stuff feelings deep inside where no one could hurt me again. Consequently, I set up my home in the pit and had believed it was the only place I deserved.

But friend, I want to pause and speak to you about your mental health. If this rings true for you, I urge you to seek professional help regardless of your faith background— Christians and people who are experiencing Jesus for the first time. Our minds are beautifully complex, but trauma, coping with hard life circumstances, and mental illness are serious conditions you don't have to fight alone. You may need help for a season, with therapy and medication under the care of a trained professional. Finally, if you are suffering from hopelessness and have thoughts of self-harm, please, friend, call the free U.S. suicide hotline at 1-800-273-8255 and start your path for renewed hope today.[15] I pray you feel the courage to take a vulnerable step today if you feel that nudge to find deeper healing. I promise God will be alongside you.

Gosia's assurance about sharing was right, but little did I know how much power and freedom the Lord would unleash in me through his pursuit to heal my heart. And it began with a *yes* to share my story. His power was in me, but until then I didn't believe he could restore me. Where was the good from it? Was he there in the ugliness of my pain? Did he look at me with love? Yes. Compassion? Yes. Righteous anger for sin and the brokenness it caused? Yes. I had believed he just stood at a distance, eyes covered, ashamed of me. I had felt abandoned by God during my darkest days of depression with gut-wrenching sobs no one saw or heard.

Pastor Marek's invitation to share my testimony was God's hand reaching down to lift me from the muck of the past. The truth came flooding in: I was free and redeemed in Christ. I thought, "Is this what it looks like to trust him? To stand unashamed for being so lost until I found the tender love of Jesus?"

Until Poland, I didn't know the power of the gospel over my story. I just buried the ugly parts deep down, except maybe to Jesus and Andrés, and tried to believe I was loved and forgiven by being "good enough." I always wanted my testimony to be about how good I was and how I was healed without professional help, then I got even more awesome because of Jesus! But it is not my story, by God's grace. It's a lot more about how ugly, lost, and broken I was, yet God still loved me and called me into his love story of redemption. Maybe this isn't your story, but I do know this kind of striving is too big of a burden to bear in a world ridden with sin and darkness. God longed for me to come to him, just as I was. In Poland, he showed me just how far he'd chase me to redeem me and show me his true heart. Instead of me rescuing myself from the pit—which I couldn't—Jesus did. My story wasn't meant to have me as the hero in the spotlight, but instead as a mirror, to reflect his love and grace in my life.

In the four years leading up to my time in Poland, God began assuaging my cognitive dissonance of what I used to believe about him, and who he was revealing himself to be: trustworthy, loving, and present. Jesus was proud when I surrendered to him changing my heart by proclaiming my testimony. I didn't need a perfectly crafted story. What I needed was my own imperfect one to set me free. The truth let me see his good grace amidst the suffering. Others needed to see my pain, so they may have hope in Jesus through their own struggles. I could hear the shouts of heaven as if the Lord were leaning over the rails to cheer me on in this brave declaration.

Therefore, since we are surrounded by such a great cloud of witnesses, let us throw off everything that hinders and the sin that so easily entangles. And let us run with perseverance the race marked out for us, fixing our eyes on Jesus, the pioneer, and perfecter of faith. For the joy set before him he endured the cross, scorning its shame, and sat down at the right hand of the throne of God. Hebrews 12:1-2

With his persistent love, the Lord was calling me to braver things. My mind had been stuck believing I was less than, left out, and hiding behind good behavior to get approval and shallow affirmation. I didn't know how to be the truest version of myself. And God was graciously inviting me to freedom when I opened up about the darkest parts of my past. But I couldn't step out of my mental prison until I acknowledged isolation had kept me in chains. Bondage wasn't where God wanted me. It grieved him to see me balled up in my cell. As soon as I cried out to him for freedom, he stepped in and ripped the door off its hinges. For the first time in my life, I believed God had more for my story by sharing it with others. I took one brave step beyond the barred walls, grabbing hold of his precious, nail-scarred hand.

My worst fears were obliterated when I chose to be honest with others about my brokenness and God's faithful pursuit of my heart. He surrounded me with a community pouring out his love, encouragement, and prayers for healing. I saw how he loved me more than I imagined. He gave me this sweet church who cried along with me at the brokenness and then celebrated how Jesus met me at my worst and is still rewriting my story.

It was the start of being masterfully mended back together, and in the seams of restoration, Jesus' hope radiated through me.

Just after my testimony on May 15, 2016. I
was beaming with a new purpose for my life.
I knew my story needed to be shared.

Spring 2016
Słupsk, Poland

A Walk in the Forest

CHAPTER 7

Towering green canopies stretched over me, I followed their smooth gray trunks to the ground where roots seemed to grow for miles below. Green moss covered them as a well-tailored velvet glove. They've taken many years to become these giants. "What are your stories, trees? How have you weathered so many storms and seasons of life?"

It was on these solitary walks through the forest in Słupsk I started to feel the voice of God beckon to my heart, "Come, let your roots spread, let them grow in me. Winds of your past have tried to break you, but you're not beyond my hope, precious daughter. I am making you anew. I will strengthen and uphold you. You will be like a tree planted by streams of water; whatever you do will prosper, you will bear much fruit in season. Just come," he offered his hand. "Dig deep into my Word and allow yourself to be enveloped in my presence. I am surrounding you. Come, let us walk together."

"But blessed is the one who trusts in the Lord, whose confidence is in him. They will be like a tree planted by the water that sends its roots by the stream. It does not fear when heat comes; its leaves are always green. It has no worries in a year of drought and never fails to bear fruit." Jeremiah 17:7-8

For most of my life, I felt stuck in a perpetual winter. Much of my childhood left me with things that seemed dead. My soul often ached but found solace alone in the stillness of nature.

Throughout my early life, I had felt disappointed, hurt, rejected, and criticized. I wanted a place to fit in and belong, but I wore a cloak of shame. A covering taunting me, "You can't tell them how you really feel," or they'll say, "You're gross," "weird," or "ugly." At school, I remember sitting on the tire swing, watching classmates happily run by as if I was invisible.

There were glimpses of goodness, some of my favorite childhood memories were playing with my cousins. When summer came, we floated in the pool for hours laughing and playing. We jumped in the hay from the second story of the barn and chased sheep through the pasture. I begged my parents to let me stay longer to enjoy these rare moments of being a kid. But even my closest cousins didn't know my feelings or deepest shames.

In my early twenties, after I returned to the Lord, I still battled hard seasons. Anxiety and depression stalked me, ready to pounce on any hope and drag me back down to the pit. Blizzards of shame buried me. I climbed my way out with performance, exercise, good friends, and nuggets of God's Word. But then another storm blew through and shook my weak footing: fights with Andrés, rejection from a close friend, constant internal battles with my past sin. My soul churned under the weight of pain and restlessness, leaving me exhausted. I couldn't do enough to satisfy my soul. Living with an unbalanced mind, I couldn't keep myself from slipping into the pit.

On unexpected occasions, when my internal chaos was still enough to hear the Lord's voice, a whisper of hope rose up from my soul.

I was made for more.

I kept striving to obey God and seek him, but he seemed distant, giving a faint "yes" or an occasional "no". Never did I seek his love, or believe he even liked me. Let alone ask, "What dreams do you have for me, Lord?" I felt alone and cold, plodding along through snowdrifts trying to please him, staying on a path that didn't satisfy me. Where else could I go? Was this the "abundant" Christian life?

I was a sapling in my faith, weighed down with snow and ice on my feeble branches. Would spring ever come and bring buds of hope? I didn't believe I would blossom, flourish, and bear sweet blessings of fruit. Nor did I understand my fruit's beauty would be *because* of the suffering and the mark it left on my heart, not despite it. It would be so much sweeter because I survived despite the odds. I would actually be fruitful because the suffering had changed my heart forever and I surrendered to the Lord's redemptive hand. I was done trying to find pleasure and satisfaction from worldly things: relationships, success, control. Nothing was powerful enough to melt the numbness in my soul. I was ready to find delight in the day-to-day and get to know Jesus as a friend. I felt I was made to be known and loved by him. Only he could satisfy my soul's deepest yearnings, heal my heart, and bring growth from what seemed cold and hopeless.

But before the trauma, before many lies and shame bombarded me, my mom recalls a time when my tiny soul rejoiced. Rolling down a New England country road in the Volkswagen Vanagon, I piped up from the back, "Mommy, look at all the green!" Spring had sprung in a magnificent canopy of oak and maple leaves bursting outside the windows.

God was speaking delight over me since I was little, falling in love with the forest.

When I started to know God and believe I was loved, I could go back in time and see the ways he was present throughout my life. I can now see how he was with me as a girl, wandering through the quiet of a fresh snowfall. I loved exploring alone and marveling at the soft glittering blanket and the stillness of the branches stretching out over me. He was with me even in the deep winter. I know God covered me with his presence and protection while he waited for me to mature before I could address the most traumatic experiences of my childhood. He knew I would return to him, back in the forest.

As the Earth warmed to spring in Poland, God brought green buds of hope to my life. He entreated me to delight in his presence in the peace of the forest, and for the first time, I truly felt his Spirit stirring and I could clearly discern his voice. The heavy burdens were lifted as he spoke life to my cold, dry bones, and drew out joy and peace. He delighted in me and loved me as I was, a new green shoot learning to trust in his love.

Jesus and I shared more walks than I can count in the beautiful forest of European beech and pine trees nestled behind my Polish home. Rain or shine, I entered their out-stretched green arms. Some days the forest was a shortcut to Katie's for dinner, a way to exercise or to recharge from a hectic workday. The trail had a particular scent of rich, damp soil woven with wood fires from nearby homes. Only the occasional jogger or speed walker with poles (I still don't understand those for flat terrain), would pass by me on those walks.

Jesus also gave me a couple of furry goat friends, Billy and Bob, who lived near the halfway point of the walking paths. I gave them these honorary names, Billy, because I saw him and thought "Billy-goat," and then Bob for the nice alliteration. They would light up and run toward me to lean in for a back scratch and handfuls of fresh grass through the fence. Billy looked deep into my eyes as if Jesus was looking into my soul from this goofy four-legged friend. He saw me.

God surprised me with delight in those trees: an elusive red squirrel with bunny-like ears scurrying through the branches, a deer peacefully grazing, and I will never forget the beautiful songbirds. The forest shouted his praise! I was refreshed by the chorus of his creation; my own heart sang in harmony with all of them.

I started listening to motivational podcasts with new-found belief and hope for my life. The Ziglar Show became my favorite, the podcasts were packed full of biblical truth to equip me for the day and get my mind in the right place. I could really believe God had more for me! I started to expect great things from my Father who was gently leading me along his right paths. *You are not your past failures;* Jesus spoke into my deepest shame.

On Sundays, I walked several kilometers and poured out my heart to Jesus. I prayed. I cried. I literally called out loud and claimed truth and victory over my life and my loved ones. Dusk crept in, the green leaves and needles settled in for the night. I feared no evil—wild boar, human, spirit or otherwise—I just kept on the path, kept praying.

The reasons for beginning a walk in the forest varied, sometimes it was motivated by wanting to hit my 10,000 steps, but truly the deeper ache was to rest in the presence of God as I acknowledged my feelings, hopes, and worries. I always left fulfilled in my spirit, mind, and body. Every day my heart yearned for my timber hideaway, for the quiet assurance of his love.

Even while working on base I slipped in a morning walk in the small forest along the main fence. That walk was dedicated prayer time to love on two people and pray aloud for them for 30 consecutive days. "Lord, help me to love Rebekah better. Help me to see the special talents and skills you've equipped her to use. Prepare her heart for her future husband, and prepare his heart for hers. And Lord, most of all let her grow in you and your love." "God, thank you for giving me sweet friendship with Iulia and giving her the courage to leave behind her past and family in Romania to start a bold new life for you in the States. Equip her for the calling you have for her life."

I prayed for restoration over the old Nazi soil. God's Spirit spoke love into and through me. "Move these people, Lord. Let them know the freedom and love that only comes from you," I prayed for Słupsk's revival. The Lord was strengthening me like one of the towering beauties in the forest. I saw a renewed purpose for his people and felt a desire to discover his plan for my life. He was alongside me every step, leaning in to hear my heart's desires.

They will be called oaks of righteousness, a planting of the Lord for the display of his splendor. Isaiah 61:3b

I found Jesus in Poland, in the quiet of the forest.

Suddenly, I realized the stillness in my heart was the Lord's gift to me, and a way he spoke to me. As I walked and prayed in my beloved Polish woods, he freed me from seeing his Word as a list of rules I had to obey to earn his acceptance and love. Instead, he showed me the Bible is a powerful tool to reveal his character.

His love letters. Written to his treasured daughter.

Take delight in the Lord, and he will give you the desires of your heart. Psalm 37:4

God loved me so much he wanted me to know him intimately, to enjoy him, to love him, to have a relationship with him. But first, and foremost to be loved by him. I struggled to understand how to love the Lord, and especially how he could love me. He previously felt elusive as I was burdened with seasons of crippling depression and the sin of performing for affirmation. I couldn't love myself, others, or the Lord until I felt safe in his love for me. Just as a child cannot thrive without a secure attachment to their caretakers, I first had to see God meeting my physical and emotional needs to rest in his love. As he reminded me of his faithfulness giving me a loving church community, multiplying my financial blessings, and quelling my loneliness, my heart was softened to his fatherly care. He did see me, his beautiful daughter.

> *And he passed in front of Moses, proclaiming, "The Lord, the Lord, the compassionate and gracious God, slow to anger, abounding in love and faithfulness."*
> Exodus 34:6

Before Poland, if you were to ask me what the first character trait, I'd use to describe God, I promise it would not be "compassionate." However, that is exactly the first word the Lord used for himself after he created a loving, protective agreement with his people, the Israelites, in the Bible. The meaning in Hebrew is also related to the word womb, showing God's nurturing care. [16] I felt his nurturing Spirit meet me in the woods and recreate my child-like wonder. He drew me in close, looked me in the eyes, and treasured who I was. I felt his joy and peace in my heart as I literally walked and built our relationship in the forest, my personal sanctuary.

> *I instruct you in the way of wisdom*
> *and lead you along straight paths.*
> *When you walk, your steps will not be hampered;*
> *when you run, you will not stumble.*
> Proverbs 4:11-12

Aching for freedom from my harsh inner critic, God paved the way for my heart to receive his Word and revelations of love. I wanted to know God's heart and he was my priority. He led me humbly into his presence. I was desperate for him to comfort my loneliness, heal my depression, and give me rest. My faith grew expecting to hear him speak with every walk. He spoke hope into my life as I sensed him coming alongside me.

Blessed are those who listen to me,
watching daily at my doors,
waiting at my doorway.
Proverbs 8:34

I welcomed him and found deep satisfaction as I let him nourish my mind with his Word and presence. Sometimes his voice came as a verse that popped into my mind, perfectly applicable to my day, other times as a profound thought that hit my heart. Those revelations were packed full of wisdom, abundantly more than I could ever reason with my twenty-seven-year-old mind. His Spirit emboldened me to speak truth and love to myself, Andrés, and my new Polish friends. I was not ashamed or fearful of how I would be perceived as a "church girl" or "super religious." God's love changed me and I couldn't help but share the overflow with others.

He guides the humble in what is right
and teaches them his way.
Psalm 25:9

Called. I was being called by Jesus. In my sweet spring season, in my forest. I was called to know his heart for me and to find myself in him.

From the depths of my soul I knew this was where God wanted me to be; walking with him. To abide in his love, his Word, and love others through the outpouring he lavished on me. I had unshakable hope for my life and experienced the soul-nurturing love of Jesus. He was gentle, knowing I was but a sprout, longing to finally delight in the day he laid before me. I kept seeking, and he kept giving me more and more of his beautiful heart.

Then you will call on me and come and pray to me, and I will listen to you. You will seek me and find me when you seek me with all your heart. Jeremiah 29:12-13

My purpose in life shifted: it wasn't about *doing* things for Jesus but *being* with him as I let him work through me. How could I bring Jesus to others if I didn't know him myself? I couldn't produce my own peace and love apart from him. Just as the trees I passed sprouted seeds in the right season, nourished by the Earth, I too realized I was meant to flourish by being connected and rooted in the goodness of God. I understood spiritual fruit to be the result of love, and not the goal. Surrendering to Jesus' invitation, I felt surrounded by his peace radiating around and through me. My inner voice hushed and the symphony of nature was amplified. God's stir in my heart sang as perfect lyrics over it all. I was swept up in the delight of being captured in the present moment. Each walk brought deeper intimacy with him, and my heart cried, "Yes!"

Dainty pink and yellow wildflowers decorated the dirt road along the fence. I tenderly stooped down to gather a bunch for my desk. A reminder of my heart walks with Jesus, and that he's always ready to take my hand and whistle joyfully through the trees.

Summer 2016
Słupsk, Poland

Nazi Hangar to House of God

CHAPTER 8

"We are believing God can provide 120,000 złoty for the next payment by the 25th!" Gosia translated for her father, Marek, as he proclaimed his vision to the church just weeks before the deadline. His faith was palpable; we knew it would be done. It was a large sum of money for the thirty or so members. Despite a typical Polish weekly paycheck being 2,000 zł ($500), the church inherently trusted God.

A few weeks later, we praised God; the exact amount needed was given. I witnessed God's ceaseless financial blessings to the Rivers of the Living Water Christian Centre throughout my time in Poland. God not only blessed the typical Sunday offerings, but people across the world called Marek and felt led to give to God's vision for this community. The Spirit was moving beyond borders to make it happen. His love was spreading like wildfire in this broken city through this little church with unstoppable hope!

God was stirring hearts in Słupsk and rapidly multiplied the church's finances to purchase a "new" building. It would seat hundreds, have a Christian school, cafe, and an inexpensive clothing shop to minister to the needs of the community. The building had the potential to be beautiful, reviving its arched windows and adding a new balcony to wrap around the sanctuary. Light would stream through the lobby to infuse an atmosphere of hope. Lives would be changed for eternity as they heard the gospel and experienced transformation by Jesus Christ's love and power.

The building on Grottgera Street was new to the church but had been vacant and derelict for almost two decades. Starting in the 1960s, it was an athletic training facility for Czarni Słupsk, "Black Słupsk", the local professional basketball team. (And while I was in Poland, the team still existed, but had difficulty with a financial scandal). The building also had a period of abandonment, before Nazis used it in WWII to store aircraft, and bombers were sent from there to destroy other Polish cities. Then long before that, its original purpose was an airplane hangar built by the Germans in 1914 as they occupied Poland. Talk about a compilation of dejected, dark, vile purposes.

But God, in his beautiful story of redemption from ruins, began to breathe life into this wasteland, reclaiming a place of hate for a house of love for his glory.

"Forget the former things;
do not dwell on the past.
See I am doing a new thing!
Now it springs up; do you not perceive it?

*I am making a way in the wilderness
and streams in the wasteland."*
Isaiah 43:18-19

His Spirit, like streams of living water, was washing over Słupsk and the transformation did not go unnoticed. The local media was abuzz. It was a miracle the church purchased the building for a fraction of its worth, and they were selected over other interested buyers. Some said the property was valued more than four times the agreed price. We prayed and praised God through the negotiations and into major construction to reclaim its broken past.

The first Saturday the church had possession of the building, half a dozen guys gathered to begin cleaning. Gosia and I joined for the last hour after running club (Biegam bo Lubię). Preparing for battle with the grime, I donned my steel toed-boots, safety glasses, gloves, and a dust mask.

It seemed insurmountable: scattered papers, broken furniture, glass shards from squatters, and building debris in every room, hall, and open space.

But Pastor Marek had a plan. We focused on one room at a time, gathering garbage and placing it into bags that were then piled in a heap by the front arched entryway. At the time, the visionary beautiful facade had several broken windows, military camouflage netting draped across it, and rusting wrought iron gates. The basement had severe flood damage and dangerous debris. Gosia and I cleaned rooms, climbed under dusty bleachers, hauled bags and damaged office electronics to be thrown out. It was hard work. The trash pile consumed much of the hangar.

More than 10 years prior, the church received a prophecy telling them not to fear the condition of the building. And as I witnessed, Pastor Marek was unflappable. Instead, he was joyful and steadfast amidst the clutter and mess. Jesus' peace was pouring out of him! I can still hear him laughing with joy and saying, "Alleluja!"

On one of my trips to the trash mountain, two men I didn't recognize arrived, looking curious, and carrying a video camera. Marek spoke with them. Gosia kindly explained to me, "These men are from a regional news station in Gdansk. Many are interested and hopeful about the renovations of this old Słupsk landmark."

Marek had a captive audience and spoke the truth with conviction and kindness about the church and the gospel. A beam of hope spread through the city and into northern Poland that day. The video crew stayed and captured the rubble and us bringing more to the growing dump. I quietly smiled, not uncovering my limited Polish. Could they tell I was a foreigner? My first (and only) Polish TV debut: a content worker helping bring new life to this building.

Soon after the camera crew left, Marek declared we had worked enough for the day; it was time to rest. I found it odd—there was so much more to do! He pragmatically said, "OK, let's go." And we did. He showed me the importance of balancing work and rest and trusting God's perfect timing. Without much explanation, he showed me how to have peace over what was done and peace leaving the rest for another day. For much of my life, I had been a hard worker to the point of burn out. Marek, like my wise Heavenly Father, called us to pause and appreciate our efforts and trust it was enough.

Once after our Saturday cleaning, one of the guys decided he wanted to be baptized. We rejoiced and Pastor Marek brought us down to a large park in the city center. Our small parade passed Soviet-era block apartments with window boxes bursting with vibrant flowers. We paused in a grassy expanse by the Słupia River. Birds sang. We praised. We prayed. Then Marek and the young man waded down the lush riverbanks into the water. Soft rain and gray skies were no match for our celebration. To my recollection, they did not have any dry clothes or towels, but it did not stop them. It was simple. Obey promptly, and much joy would follow.

I saw God move; he was in the business of restoring ruins—buildings and hearts alike.

I was overjoyed to witness God's powerful work in this church and with these believers. They were like family and their hope was contagious. I loved supporting them with my tithe and volunteered time. It humbled me to see the building in its abandoned state—disposed of, forgotten, broken. I was strengthened believing God had the vision and power to restore it. He chose this space for the church, to strengthen our trust and draw the lost and broken to his heart.

After I returned home, people from the base were still connected with the church. A group of young men regularly volunteered to help Pastor Marek with demolition and reconstruction. Amazingly, but not surprisingly, the Lord used members of the American military, on their own time, to help rebuild this church. Long before the building was obtained, Pastors Marek and Ala received a prophetic message that said, "People of many nations will help you build this church." And so it was.

While renewing the church, I witnessed God building his kingdom one day at a time, one life at a time. Pastor Marek encouraged us often, "our church's size doesn't matter—it's about our faithfulness to the covenant [relationship with Jesus] that we can do so much more." Marek reminded us of the story in Nehemiah when Jerusalem was being rebuilt by a tiny group of people in 52 days. He proclaimed "It's not about our size. It's about God's power and size! [We] can't get stuck on human scales. [He's] bigger than our dreams. God wants his kingdom to grow!" [17]

"Stretch out your hand to heal and perform signs and wonders through the name of your holy servant Jesus." After they prayed, the place where they were meeting was shaken. And they were all filled with the Holy Spirit and spoke the word of God boldly.
Acts 4:30-31

And thanks be to God, who invited us to participate in his work. I felt confident God placed each of us in the church in that season to serve and build up his house. We saw this building as a wonderful tool God gave us to reach more people. Pastor Ala and Marek were faithful in the small things for more than a decade, and God chose that moment to expand their ministry. They had such a deep love for Jesus, their humble presence exuded God's love. Their heart was to share Christ's love with the city by meeting the practical needs of the community.

I was overjoyed seeing God provide for the church and humbly grateful to be part of the Lord's longing to revive Słupsk and the nation. I experienced what the mighty power of the Lord could do when we, as a church, earnestly sought him with unshakable trust, then acted on his calling for us. "We were called to live in power, authority, and live out [God's] will for our life," Marek encouraged us.[17] The genuine passion and faith Pastors Marek and Ala had was contagious.

God spoke hope into my life. *You are made for more, daughter.* My calling wasn't to be a "good Christian" but to join him on an amazing adventure of bringing his kingdom and love to Earth. Each day, I began waking up and asking, "What are you up to, today, Jesus?" and sensed his presence around me. He invited me to come alongside him and see his heart bring hope to the broken, lost things of this world.

> *He has saved us and called us to a holy life—not because of anything we have done but because of his own purpose and grace. This grace was given us in Christ Jesus before the beginning of time, 2 Timothy 1:9*

My role in bringing Jesus' love to people in Słupsk was small, but I found purpose and inexpressible fulfillment from serving. I didn't need to work to please God. I got to participate in the work, it was an honor and joy to share the love that was lavishly given to me. I was encouraged to come alongside other believers who shared their own stories of transformation from the moment they recognized God at work in their lives.

> *And he who was seated on the throne said, "Behold, I am making all things new!" Then he said, "Write this down, for these words are trustworthy and true."* Revelation 21:5

God still works miracles; the ugliest parts of our past and darkest parts of human history aren't beyond his redemption. He loved us before we knew him. When we act boldly in faith and trust his promises, we bring his kingdom to minister to the world's greatest needs, one heart at a time. When it seems impossible, Jesus steps in and resurrects with new life, new hope, a new purpose.

And my heart was about to encounter how he would do the miraculous for me.

Inside the church's "new" main
auditorium: the garbage heap.

May 21, 2016
Słupsk, Poland

Ancient Ruins Restored

CHAPTER 9

> *"Your people will rebuild the ancient ruins*
> *and will raise up the age-old foundations;*
> *you will be called Repairer of Broken Walls,*
> *Restorer of Streets with Dwellings."*
> Isaiah 58:12

Northern Poland's countryside has endless rolling hills and open farmland. In the late spring, I saw delicate yellow and cornflower-blue blossoms covering the land. Puffy clouds floated above me in the blue sky and contrasted with the vibrant fields. Old trees stood guard along narrow roads. Villages had cozy homes with brick chimneys, terra cotta tile roofs, and an occasional stork nest on a powerline pole dotted the landscape. Strolls through my neighborhood brought me delight as I saw metal garden gates hem in brightly painted houses with burgeoning rose bushes. In the city, geraniums—vibrant reds and pinks—framed the balconies of Soviet-era mid-rise apartments along with the day's laundry. Centuries-old brick churches, walls, gates, and a medieval witch tower had patched battle scars after the devastation from the great world wars.

I felt hope bursting forth from the country's broken past. Life from death. Beauty from ashes. The architecture was steadfast and wise as it had weathered many generations of suffering and deliverance. Grime in stucco cracks was dressed up with fine lace-curtained windows and potted plants. I had hope for these ancient ruins.

I looked within myself and saw a tired, cracked facade riddled with pain and shame from my past. Where was my beauty? Where was my deliverance?

God was planting hope in my life. His love was blossoming through this spring season to clean my grimy cracks and ill-placed boundaries in my mind. He approached the walls I set to protect myself from pain like trailing ivy, continually growing upward, reaching for my heart. I paused to notice the facade I had built up around my seemingly hopeless past to disguise my brokenness.

The Lord didn't discard my ruins or allow me to have amnesia about my past, instead, he lovingly reframed struggles one by one and used them for my restoration. I wasn't a hopeless case. He gave me renewed purpose and affirmed my inner beauty was being magnified by the pain and suffering I was overcoming. But I couldn't fully appreciate my restoration until I finally acknowledged the biggest ruins: depression, sexual abuse, manipulation, fear, self-hatred. I needed to stop covering up the ugliness from my past and accept my brokenness on this side of eternity. I needed to let God into the walls of my heart.

From childhood, I had grown accustomed to hiding from my parents, from friends, and especially from God about my feelings and broken circumstances. I thought my lies worked; no one seemed to care or notice there was more to my sensitive heart. In a way, the lies worked. When I wasn't honest, I diminished my chance of being seen. Lies choked the capacity of my mind to believe otherwise, my mindset was fixed. It was how I survived—*throw on enough paint and they can't see the dirt.* My cover-ups included high performance at school, withdrawal and repressing my thoughts and feelings, and lots of lying to please others. I believed I could be fulfilled and happy "if only I could control this person, if only I could erase my past, if only I went to this school." I wanted to run from who I thought I was. I needed a fresh start. I had hoped to escape when I started college.

But my first year at Clarkson was a shock to my plan. For the first time in my life, I failed exams, received C's on my transcript, and believed I wasn't smart enough to figure out homework on my own. I heaped on damage with an unhealthy romantic relationship. My brain was drowning in pressure from depression, anxiety, and perfectionism. By spring, my relationship was dead, I had cheated on him and he had returned the favor, my grades were atrocious (by my standards), and I was falling to pieces. My circumstances seemed to confirm my beliefs: I was hopeless and unloved. At my most broken, I seriously considered taking my life and was on suicide watch in March of that year. Hospitalization was almost necessary. Something needed to change. By God's grace, I finally agreed to try medication. It soon helped manage the raging lows, but I had numbness in my soul, yearning for more from life. What was my purpose? Where was my joy? I kept running from God. Did he care? Did he even exist?

From freshman year in 2008 until the fall of 2012, while I ran, God patiently waited. I got to another place of desperation and had nowhere to turn. Andrés and I had been married almost two years at the time, and we had just moved from Los Angeles to Massachusetts. Tensions rose in our house as I self-weaned from antidepressants and was struggling to stay afloat with grad school's demands.

I didn't have space to breathe, let alone make time to be honest about my shameful past to a new therapist. I hadn't seen a counselor in over a year and my inner voice believed the lies. *Just keep painting my old, cracked facade,* I thought, *no one will know better. Keep moving forward, otherwise, you'll fall to pieces, Sarah.* And who would be there to put me back together?

God patiently kept calling me into his restorative arms. I made an unexpected friend, Matt, at my internship. He was an engineer *and* a loved Jesus. *Perhaps I could try God again. Perhaps God was real and cared about my situation.*

I felt a funny desire to buy a Bible for my Kindle. On the commuter train to Boston, I opened the Word and began in the Psalms. My eyes were opened, and my soul felt a weight lift. I soaked up the words about pain, struggle, and emotions. David had cracks in his facade, acknowledged them, and kept running after God. What if there *was* hope for me?

My walk with the Lord began more like a wobbly crawl. Sometimes before exams, I was so anxious I could vomit, forgetting the assurance of God's peace from my devotionals. In bathroom stalls and subway trains, I pleaded for peace and favorable exams. Then worship music started interjecting itself on secular stations on Pandora as I studied. In the short span of a few months, I began feeling more hopeful, less anxious, and could enjoy life.

During that time, Andrés' favorite uncle and mentor, Tío Guillermo, passed away suddenly. He had great faith, was always one for funny stories, and had lived an intentionally slow-paced life with his sweet bride, Sue, and their four adult children and families. Andrés' heart was softened, and he thought we should start going to church and follow his uncle's loving example. Until then, I had kept much of my blossoming curiosity about God quiet from him. What if he rejected me? *Another person to leave me,* I feared. But God was working in his heart too. We began attending Mass together, a compromise church service where we both felt comfortable.

I still had issues, but the Lord was lightening my load. Now I realize I could have grown faster if I had sought therapy, but God met me in the small work and taught me himself day by day with devotionals and podcasts. In my heart, I knew I didn't want to depend on antidepressants for a lifetime if it wasn't medically necessary. I didn't have shame associated with needing them; the deep wounds of my past were beyond the healing the medication could provide. I didn't just need healing from my current anxiety and depression, I needed to know in my heart of hearts I was loved and seen, and that my broken story was not beyond repair.

For a few years, I kept choosing God in my daily life. I had an earnest desire to know him and find inner peace. I experienced growing glimpses of his healing—writing letters forgiving my abusers and asking for forgiveness from those I abused. One day I delivered a letter and the recipient set it down, unopened, and embraced me. God's love unraveled my soul when I chose to courageously obey the nudge to write it; I would have never imagined such love and grace. A burden of my past shame was released. In his goodness, God knew.

Oftentimes, I sang alone and unashamed in my kitchen—hands held high in awe of God's love for me. I desired to fill my mind with Word and biblical podcasts. God even sustained our marriage, insulating me from rejection from Andrés' internal concerns about my growing "crazy religiousness," and prevented him from seriously considering divorce.

In 2015, I was baptized by my childhood pastor and God brought family all over the east coast to celebrate including all four of my grandparents, my mom, Andrés, aunts, uncles, and cousins, and our closest friends. I shared part of my testimony that day, but carefully crafted it not to embarrass or shame others for my traumatic childhood. Nor was I ready to step into my fully redeemed identity and withheld the full truth in my own shame. Jesus knew I would one day, and following his lead was like wading into a lake; my toes squished mud, then water up to my knees, and finally my waist. Eventually, my thoughts stopped focusing on the murky pond. I plunged, entirely, and was raised with new life. Up to that point, my baptism day was the greatest, joy-filled day I had experienced. Why? It was founded on Jesus.

But I was still chained by deeply ingrained lies as I kept much of these thoughts to myself. Was I truly forgiven? Was I really loved? Where was the promised abundant life?

I came to Poland at 27, only four years after I reaffirmed my commitment to follow Jesus. He kept pursuing me despite the wall of lies I had built that kept me from experiencing his love and joy. Brick by brick, I tried to hide and protect my wounded heart in response to my traumatic past, but Jesus only broke the wall down when I asked him to help. He did not force his love on me but mercifully waited for me to invite him in. And I was ready.

I see you, Sarah. I've always seen you. In Słupsk, Jesus answered my plea and broke down lies to free me to live fulfilled in the truth of his love. Scripture came alive to me, especially as I meditated on Isaiah 61 and Psalms 1, 23, 40, and 103. I heard God's Spirit speak to my heart, and I joyfully wanted to know him better.

God's Spirit was alive and moving in Słupsk. He not only was restoring my life but working to rebuild the city. He stirred my heart to love the people of Poland, his people. Once only known to my ignorant self as the brunt of bad jokes, I began to have a love for this nation beyond my comprehension. I had compassion for the man at the bar at seven in the morning looking to escape. My heart was moved for the elderly woman, deep lines of the past carved into her face as she sold me flowers for 2 zł. (~$0.50) every Friday at the farmer's market. I eagerly looked for the elderly man on the corner of my walking route who would strike up a conversation with me. *Let them know you, Jesus, and be transformed by your love. Let your love flow through me,* I prayed.

Hope rose as I frequented the cobbled paths and prayed. I thought everyone could sense new beginnings. God opened my eyes when a coworker and friend described Słupsk as "grungy" and "depressing", discouraging my love for the city and its people. Perhaps it was partially true, but I could see beauty unfolding. I was not stuck in the seen world and had a vision of what God was to bring from these ruins. Beautiful hope was in the space between now and not yet—the perfect place for miracles.

He spoke to me, *my daughter, I am doing the same thing for your life. You see it for these people, believe it for yourself. I see you, beautiful, and trust I know how you will shine when I fully restore you.*

For the first time, I welcomed Jesus' presence and heard and believed all his promises for me. His love and power to transform my life were palpable. My ancient ruins were his canvas to rebuild his redemption story. I was not as beautiful as I covered myself up from shame. Unexpectedly, I found I was beautiful when I embraced the broken because Christ was shining out through my fissures I had desperately tried to cover. I began to believe my past no longer defined me. I was beautiful as I reflected God's goodness in my life. My worn facade, a broken woman, humble, rebuilt on his love. I looked at myself and saw good. I saw hope. I saw life from death. I saw God do the impossible in my broken heart and set me on a firm foundation of love and transform the most hopeless ruins.

They will rebuild the ancient ruins
and restore the places long devastated;
they will renew the ruined cities

108

that have been devastated for generations.
Isaiah 61:4

And the beautifully good news is Jesus loves you too. Your past is not too far gone for his miraculous love. Let him rebuild your broken places, let him love you.

Farewell to Blanket (an embarrassing story)

Friend, I have to tell you something. I had a blankie. It was white and had buttery-soft waffle fabric with pastel balloons, at least for the first few years of my life. I hated it when my mom washed my precious protector. I clung to it through so many storms. In elementary school, I'd bring it with me, hidden in my backpack on the entryway with dozens of other bags and jackets. During breaks, I'd sneak out a corner of it and get a big sniff of comfort. My teacher, Mrs. W., never seemed to question my suspicious activity.

It came with me to college. I hid it in my pillowcase from my roommates. It came with me when I moved in with Andrés; I had to tell him the truth about my other love. He called it a rag but knew I literally adored it to pieces. It even journeyed with me to Ecuador when I met my future in-laws. I had promised myself, "Ok, when I get married, I won't need it." Our wedding came and went, but blankie stayed cozy in my arms.

My mom knew I still had it and she would pester me, "Aren't you going to get rid of that thing?" But I held it even tighter, though I had terrible shame about it. *I shouldn't need this.* But it had sopped up countless rivers of tears and seen me at my worst. Who knew me better than my blanket? *No one*, I thought.

But then I packed for Poland, gave it a ceremonious sniff and I left it behind. I knew it had to stay. When I came home for a week in July 2016, I gingerly laid it to rest in a storage bin under my bed. My soul didn't need it anymore. I had found a much better comforter: Jesus. Now it may seem trite, but my blanket literally was a coping mechanism through the trauma of childhood and adolescence. By God's grace, my desire for my blankie vanished. My heart was changed as I had grown exponentially in those four months apart. My depression was gone, I had hope for my immediate and eternal future. I believed I was treasured and was fearfully and wonderfully made. [18] I felt comfortable being me. God brought me into his chest and smoothed my hair, I knew he would continue to hold me through all my storms. I was truly restored, and praise Jesus, I still am.

A tremendous turning point on my healing journey came only weeks after I found my beloved Polish church. Gosia invited me to come to hear the testimony of Pastor Artur Ceronski and attend his guest message at the church. Roy and I went together, walking through the city in the warm spring air. My spirit anticipated a breakthrough. Just the week prior I found freedom as I shared my testimony.

Pastor Artur had a powerful story—one of murder, drugs, and prison and how he had a personal encounter with Jesus after reading the Bible out of boredom in his prison cell. His heart was transformed and God gave him the gift of teaching. He taught his prison mates, and then upon release, became a pastor. He didn't sound like a typical pastor, according to Gosia who translated. Artur was punchy and sometimes raw. When I met him, he preached on how to "Build a foundation for a personal relationship with the Lord," and it mirrored what God was inviting me to as well, to see ruins repaired and my life set on his firm truth. Pastor Artur used John 15 as the key scripture, Jesus said:

> *"My command is this: Love each other as I have loved you. Greater love has no one than this: to lay down one's life for one's friends. You are my friends if you do what I command. I no longer call you my servants, because a servant does not know his master's business. Instead, I have called you friends, for everything that I learned from my Father I have made known to you. You did not choose me, but I chose you and appointed you so that you might go and bear fruit—fruit that will last—and so that whatever you ask in my name the Father will give you."* John 15:12-16

Two hearts grace the margins of my Bible in this passage with the note: "As a friend, get to know the author of our life, not just follow the instruction manual as a servant. Jesus is inviting us to rest in his security. Relax, and joyfully walk with the Lord! Let God love you." Jesus invited me to abide with him, be connected to him as the branches of his strong vine and see the wonders he'd do.

That night we declared by Jesus' power for my depression to leave! Pastor Artur prayed over me and rested his hand on my head, "W imię Jezusa, W imię Jezusa!" (In the name of Jesus!) Artur continued to pray. Gosia prayed. Ala prayed. Roy prayed.

And Jesus moved.

An excerpt from my journal that night burst off the pages.

Today the Lord healed my depression!

Pastor Artur preached a powerful sermon on God's love for us and how we need to ride his wave of love—not try to understand it or reject it with self-righteousness or self-loathing. He's crazy about me! He wants a deep, meaningful relationship with me. I need to constantly look for him working in all circumstances or else I end up putting myself first and I will suffer. Just because I don't understand everything God has done and will do; I can trust he has a reason. I cannot get trapped by the devil's attempts to complicate my relationship with Jesus. It's simple. He's my Lord and Savior, and I love him, and he loves me completely. Long before I stopped rejecting him, he loved me. I can't do anything to lose or gain more love from him. He sees me as beautifully blameless because Jesus already had a plan to restore my brokenness by his perfect love poured out on the cross.

[The Lord] showed his healing power over me this evening. Pastor Artur prayed over me for the depression to leave in the name of Jesus! He kept repeating it. I got weak, started coughing, and crying. I was laid out on the floor and covered with a silky royal-purple cloth. My entire body was quivering as I cried, but then I felt a warm tingling everywhere—not just my skin but

through and through. Gosia, Ala, and Roy contin-
ued to pray over me and then with me.

We spoke words of praise and healing. Ala said,
"And now you will learn to trust." God is bringing
me to a new level. He is going to show me how to
trust him. He is filling every cell in my body with
his love. I am in a deep river of God's love for me.
Praise the Lord who heals! I have a lightness in
my heart. My eyes look brighter. I am beautiful
because Christ is in me. I am his new creation!
Praise the Lord who heals and takes away my
burdens. Let his light shine brighter through me.

I felt Jesus healing my brokenness with heavenly kisses. He
energized every cell and filled me with the Spirit's strength.
A new fire was set in my heart. I could see the Lord covering
me with his protection and reinforcing my sound mind. I
finally was able to love myself as I received his love. God
was restoring me for great things and lasting beauty for his
kingdom and glory.

With my depression healed, the Lord gave me a clear
vision for his heart for those who caused me pain: love them.
Love them as he has loved me. Let them be drawn to the
throne of grace and experience the freedom and power in
Christ's love. I was set free in a moment from my depression
for the rest of my time in Poland. Sweet summer growth
was coming and my heart was bursting with hope. Jesus
delighted in the work of restoring my heart, and I know he
will continue to do the miraculous as I keep my eyes open
to his invitation to restore ancient ruins.

I adored this building along my typical walking
route—the dirt, the roughened exterior, the roofline
and its contrast with the bright blue sky, and
especially the hope of the flowering balconies.

Fall 2016/Fall 2019
Słupsk, Poland/San Luis Obispo, California

Deeper Waters

CHAPTER 10

Deep calls to deep
in the roar of your waterfalls;
all your waves and breakers
have swept over me.
Psalm 42:7

Skyscraper-high swells glittered like crystal before crashing into the beach. I grasped a perfectly smooth piece of purple sea glass and escaped the roar of the water just in time.

Awake in the stillness of my bedroom, the thrill of the hunt and the sweet ocean air lingered.

I often dream I am starting an adventure. Despite an unknown destination, I get stuck preparing for the trip. Sometimes I'm packing my home to move, sorting through endless piles to choose the right things for my new life. Other times I'm frantically throwing things in a suitcase to catch a plane or a rocket at the last minute. Ironically, when I finally arrive, I never use my luggage. Most journeys bring me to water; I stroll along beautiful beaches searching for sea glass.

Andrés often tells me "you never sit still, never rest" with an exasperated tone. Even in my dreams, I'm in a perpetual state of motion. At my worst, I move because I am terrified of rejection and am compelled to earn my worth. But at my best, God created me to be a sojourner, taking a journey to explore the depths of my heart and experience how mine perfectly fits into his. This can happen wherever he brings me—awake or asleep, in foreign nations or at home. I get stuck packing, worrying I need more than I have for what's ahead, but it's actually robbing me of the blessings of the journey. I'm slowly learning to let go of my fears of the unknown and invite the Lord to draw me deeper. Instead, I am learning to invite him to help me prepare for the places he's taking me. And once I arrive, I rest and enjoy.

Don't tell Andrés, but he was right. I do need more rest, rest in knowing God has good plans for me and he is working on my behalf. "Of course I was right!" Andrés would exclaim and laugh. "About what?"

Before Poland, I limited God to the size of my narrow mindedness and tiny dreams. My future was choked with pessimism, depression, practicality, and cultural norms of the American dream. My engineering background taught me to look for facts, conservative assumptions, and make cautious moves forward. My structural engineering career didn't have space for dreams. It was about following rules, codes, and numbers. Culturally, I was sensitive to consumerism and noticed I felt awkward and out of place after walking through a mall, believing I was ugly without the latest trends. My calendar exploded with events and causes and life seemed to hustle from one activity to the next to fill the voids of my heart. It had been all I knew.

Sarah, come, I have wonderful things for you, just ask, the Lord called through the lapping waves of the Baltic.

The Lord shook me and challenged me to release him from my box of tiny hopes.

God drew me deeper into his heart, where he slowly revealed his desires for my life. He knew my fragile heart needed assurance to build my trust after my miraculous healing. I stood on the shore and dropped my emotional baggage like deflated water wings. One brave step after another, I ventured into the dancing current.

Assuredly, I was refreshed seeing the Lord move and notice his goodness surrounding me. The Holy Spirit's power was stirring my heart to get past my comfort zone of shallow waves. *Come, wade deeper, my daughter,* God entreated me. *I have so much more for you.* Unashamed, I continued into the surf with my arms outstretched. I ached to draw closer and begin to explore how wide, high, long, and deep, like my beloved Baltic sea, is his love for me. He was filling deep wells in my soul with his love—the breakers swirled around me with his fullness. He uniquely designed me with voids in my heart to only be filled with his Spirit. I continued to invite the Lord to fill these wells after he had dredged out the poison from my suffering.

God had pursued me to Poland despite my striving, through the stress, and frequent state of being overwhelmed by my emotions. He knew my little heart. Actually, he knew it was a tremendous heart—one he specially created to receive his love and pour it into others in beautiful ways. Set free, I stopped listening to the fear drowning my God-given dreams and hopes and waded deeper.

One of those dreams was motherhood.

Andrés and I had been married for almost six years when I lived in Poland, still, we had never thought it was a good time to have children. We had demanding jobs, debt, and a social life. We didn't have a house or live in a cute neighborhood. We were busy with our careers and Andrés traveled at least one week a month. I worried kids would be a burden. I worried I'd be stuck at home bored and playing with kids on the weekends. I thought I would be isolated and alone in my caring for the children. The thought of being responsible for another human-made Andrés nervous. He also constantly told me he couldn't have a girl: He'd have a heart attack and die as soon as a boy looked at her, or he'd kill the boy and escape to the mountains of Ecuador.

I took those threats to heart and internalized them. I believed "girls aren't worth it, therefore I'm not worth it either." The enemy manipulated Andrés' words to prod at deep wounds of feeling exposed and unprotected. But now I see the truth, God allows some suffering and pain to mature me and he always gives me a way to find him in the midst. Unlike my husband's kind, but overprotective desires, God does not secure me in bubble wrap to prevent every ill thing from happening. God used my painful childhood and will use future sorrow—in a way only he could orchestrate—to draw me back to him and give me a longing for the complete restoration of my broken heart. What life throws at me never revokes the identity God gave me.

My deep-seated fear about having children was they would have the same traumas I did. I imagined my broken childhood as theirs; I was paralyzed with fear they would be abused and feel lost, hopeless, and unloved. How could I ensure it would never happen? My answer had been simple; don't have children. Then I'd never experience such pain and nor would they. Somewhere, deep in my soul, I wanted to be a mother. I wanted to raise children with Andrés.

And I couldn't even fathom the joy and delight a child would bring. For too long, the darkness of my past had marred any hope for the future. I had no idea how powerful and all-consuming love is between parent and child. The enemy couldn't stifle me any longer; God was calling me to delight in his blessings for my family.

One crisp fall morning, I pondered the Lord's invitation on my red sofa in the comfort of my cozy Polish flat. I freely expressed my fears and worries and heard his assurance.

Andrés and I were seriously considering a cross-country move to California soon after the completion of my Poland assignment. It left me feeling unanchored even before moving, worrying over raising children away from extended family and childcare planning once I returned to work. Of course, I felt obligated to work—why would I want to discard my years of school? As if it was all or nothing.

I felt God's persistence—*Do you want children? Do you want to be a mother? Can you trust me with your heart? Can you trust me with your children's future?* He knew my deepest fears better than I knew myself.

Exhaling my burdens, a passage in Isaiah came alive. His peace washed over me like a beautiful towering wave of my dreams. I wasn't afraid, instead, I felt comforted by his surrounding, powerful presence.

"When you pass through the waters,
I will be with you;
and when you pass through the rivers,
they will not sweep over you.
When you walk through the fire,
you will not be burned;
the flames will not set you ablaze.
For I am the Lord your God,
the Holy One of Israel, your Savior;
I give Egypt for your ransom,
Cush and Seba in your stead."
Isaiah 43:2-3

Waves of trouble wouldn't overtake me, but I would be secure in his all-encompassing presence. My season of motherhood would be challenging, but I knew in my heart I would not be alone. The Lord encouraged my heart, *Sarah, I am going to lead you through hard places. But it's going to be OK. Do you know why? Because I am going to be right there with you, holding you, guiding you, loving you.*

I felt the Lord promise me he would build a community of women to come alongside me, woven together with a heart for Jesus. The Lord also reminded me I had Andrés, my steady, strong husband, who was wild about me and would be a wonderful father. I started feeling hopeful for this new season and trusted God's ever-present help *without* knowing all the details.

I knew I needed to say yes and let go of my fears of the hypothetical brokenness of my future children and see all the goodness and love in my life. My hopes continued to rise as my desire for a family was greater than any lie the enemy threw at me. God was redeeming my family and I felt new peace trusting him with our stories as I continually surrendered my fears at his feet.

After my deep restoration in Poland, I can look back at my story with gratitude. I am grateful for my hard past, as it shaped me into the woman I am today. I can see good, as Joseph said to his family years after he had been sold by his brothers:

> *"You intended to harm me, but God intended it for good to accomplish what is now being done, the saving of many lives."* Genesis 50:20

I get to choose to trust the Lord to do the same with the children he gives me. Whatever trials my future children will face, I pray the Lord works to draw them to his heart for his good purposes. He is faithful to me; he will be faithful to them.

The storms raged as I returned to the States in 2016 and tried to bring me down and shake my trust in the Lord. I had a debilitating season of depression. But I kept choosing to run to Jesus. His presence felt different—quiet at times, dimmed by my pain, but I never felt abandoned. I sensed I wasn't alone in the pain. He saw me and knew, even when I couldn't express it. He knew my sorrowful, gut-wrenching sobs, cries too deep no sound escaped my mouth except gasps for air.

I begged God for deliverance; I didn't want to let my depression overtake me. I was done being numb, believing

I was unloved, living in a constant state of overwhelm by life's daily demands, done living without purpose, passion, and hope. Scriptures were my lifeline. I made a stack of sticky notes with a dozen hope-packed verses. Most mornings I claimed them aloud, knowing one day these would feel true again. Jesus was in the midst of my suffering and doubts and was still not ashamed of me. He was with me in the darkest nights, doing deep work in my heart. Could I praise him in the valleys as I had on the mountain tops? Could I draw deeper into his presence despite the torrent of emotions around me for comfort? Yes. Could he use pain to bring good and change my heart? Yes.

We moved to San Luis Obispo, California in May of 2017. Andrés chose to follow Christ whole-heartedly only a week after we arrived, on Mother's Day. God honored a dream in my heart I had had for years, that we would both love and be dedicated to Jesus before we had children, although I never explicitly prayed about it. I found a welcoming, Jesus-loving group of women to encourage me as I settled into the community and we fiercely prayed together, over our lives' hopes, struggles, and fears. A good new friend, Danae, walked with me through my pregnancy and heard my stories of Poland. New hope was rising in my heart like the golden rays of the sunrise. Then our sweet Annabelle Grace was born in the spring of the following year. We decided not to keep the gender a surprise. And did Andrés die or run away when he saw our precious gift in the hospital? No, he was overwhelmed with love and said, "Of course I wanted a daughter!

Every good and perfect gift is from above, coming down from the Father of heavenly lights, who does not change like shifting shadows. James 1:17

My heart has been undone by love for my daughter, Annabelle Grace. My Father has given me a glimpse of loving-kindness as his treasured daughter, and I will always be. It is a gift I get to receive; it is inherent to who I am: his daughter. Raising Annabelle and taking delight in her has given me new hope and healing from my own broken childhood. The Father's love surrounds me. He is calling me to delight in him once again as an innocent, loved daughter and rest in his loving embrace.

Fast-forward to now, 2019, in sunny, warm San Luis Obispo, thriving in all areas of my life. I am overwhelmed at God's faithfulness and the beauty of his unfolding promises. In a beautiful dream, we drove along the jagged coastline. Andrés was in the back seat with me. Huge waves crashed and reached the top of the cliffs. Another one came with fierce height and effortlessly engulfed us. Somehow we kept moving forward on the road. Dumbfounded I asked, "What's happening?" and the driver calmly answered, "That's how we do it around here."

Now I see the Lord like a vast ocean and the powerful waves are his Spirit. Stormy trials will not overcome me, but I can be swept up in the protection of the Lord's presence. As I have said yes to his calling on my life, he has completely inundated my life. Set free, I constantly release the lies and limiting beliefs in the roar of the surf. I've never felt such peace, love, and purpose as I've learned the daily choice to surrender my heart's longings to him.

When I received his promise from Isaiah 43 in Słupsk, I didn't understand how going through trials would lead me to enjoy his presence and draw out my calling. I wasn't even scared about what trials he would lead me through. I was fixed on Jesus and wanted to step into the waves with courage. Choppy waters and sharp, biting winds did not make me cower and sink. My brave new journey began in Poland, completely free. I stepped out and could feel his breath, feel his embrace—it didn't matter the storm as long as he had my hand.

Looking back for the last four years, I have endured hard seasons. But I realized that God's presence *is* my greatest desire. He is my peace and strength, whether I'm in the waves or fire, I get to be with him. And most beautifully, I know the Lord himself draws near and scoops me up from my pit of despair. I get to rest being with him and let him work deep in my heart.

I continued to invite the waves to come because in his presence is the safest place I could ever be and the greatest desire of my heart.

My life's prayer is that I am in a continual place of deep surrender and trust in my Father. I don't even want to have my head above water. That would imply I need some control, holding on to a few fragile things I desperately want to go well, and can't trust him to handle. The time strolling the shore is over; I don't want an ankle-deep relationship. I want a vibrant, moving, powerful life with the Spirit's undeniable beauty washing over me.

For this reason, I kneel before the Father, from whom every family in heaven and on earth derives its name. I pray that out of his glorious riches he may strengthen you with power through his Spirit in your inner being, rooted and established in love, may have power together with all the Lord's holy people, to grasp how wide and long and high and deep is the love of Christ, and to know this love that surpasses knowledge—that you may be filled to the measure of all the fullness of God. Ephesians 3:14-19

And his love is calling me deeper still.

June 2016
Słupsk, Poland

Rooted

CHAPTER 11

Weed: noun, "a valueless plant growing wild, especially one that grows on cultivated ground to the exclusion or injury of the desired crop." [19]

I learned about weeding as a preteen, earning a few dollars an hour to pluck invaders from Mrs. G's beautiful gardens. Her acreage had rolling hills, a duck pond, a two-story barn, and a regal brick colonial in the heart of the historic village of my hometown. Mrs. G. graciously joined me in the beginning, teaching me to remove the plant's root, otherwise, it would return and continue to spread.

On my knees in the sun, wearing a hot and extremely embarrassing mosquito net hat, I pulled weed after weed. The 5-gallon buckets filled quickly and I lugged them to the compost pile. I maintained several garden beds surrounding her home. Each week I visited the same garden beds, pulling new offenders, and keeping her gardens pristine. It was hard but satisfying work. A cute young man who mowed their lawns also wasn't a bad perk.

My heart found summer in Poland. I adored the glorious green fields, vibrant trees, zinnias and roses, and fragrant damp soil after drenching rains. My trust in God was in full bloom, walking in the Lord's daily purpose and hope for my life. I soaked in the goodness of nature and God's love for me in the warming rays on-site walks and strolls in the forest. One week passed with no depression, then three, then a month and more! But as any gardener knows, summer brings rapid growth of all plants—good fruit and weeds alike.

The Lord encouraged me to roll up my sleeves and dig into my emotional dirt. Ugly roots had long choked my heart, but the thick fog of depression had blinded me. Jesus met me as he had with so many people in the Gospels; first healing my physical and emotional needs and then addressing sin.

Lots of my problems centered around critical, negative thoughts. I realized I would be frustrated as I walked along the Baltic with Katie as she leash-trained her cat, Stella. It was painstakingly slow, the cat would resist, and I believed I was missing out on fantastic sea glass just beyond view. These struggles were about my inconveniences; I didn't take a moment to understand my friend's desires.

At church, I would be annoyed when Gosia would warmly greet me and ask, "Did you bring anyone today?" I felt ashamed and rationalized it would be awkward for me to invite coworkers to church. But I also sensed Gosia's genuine concern and love for me and my work friends. However, I had baggage from my past to share my faith out of obligation because it was the right thing to do. My heart churned to discern what was good and push past my comforts.

When I wore my engineering hat (a fabulous white hard-hat with a thick brim to keep the rain off my head), I would get impatient if conversations with contractors went on too long or they misunderstood me. I'd feel like their requests for information were an affront to my intelligence. I never dared to express my annoyance in any of these circumstances. Any confrontation made me sick to my stomach, I longed to keep the peace. But deep down by conviction of the Holy Spirit, I knew I was not justified with my frustrations and internal lack of peace. I continued to chew on these criticisms and let them fester. Roots of anger, pride, impatience, and selfishness were curling around my heart.

Sarah, Sarah, the Lord gently chided. *You need to let go and give them grace. Give yourself grace. Have compassion and see their heart. Rest in the day I have laid out for you, I have this in my hands. Repent, and I will free you.* The Lord was freeing me from the internal turmoil that consumed my energy and thoughts.

God's Word in Galatians 5 says:

You, my brothers and sisters, were called to be free. But do not use your freedom to indulge the flesh; rather, serve one another humbly in love...

The acts of the flesh are obvious: sexual immorality, impurity, and debauchery; idolatry and witchcraft; hatred, discord, jealousy, fits of rage, selfish ambition, dissensions, factions and envy, drunkenness, orgies, and the like. I warn you, as I did before, that those who live like this will not inherit the kingdom of God.

But the fruit of the Spirit is love, joy, peace, patience, kindness, goodness, faithfulness, gentleness, and self-control. Against such things, there is no law.
Galatians 5:13, 19-23

On a "perfect" day, when everything went according to *my* plan, contentment still evaded me! Instead, I was already thinking of the next thing I needed to do and followed my flesh. Blinded by the drive to accomplish, I was missing the beautiful relationships the Lord had given me. Repenting in my journal I wrote:

My Heavenly Father is so good to me! He is keeping my depression far away and giving me time to experience his love and power—my God is Greater!! You have lifted the fog of despair and have given me new clarity, new hope, and new joy in you. You are also allowing me to see sinful patterns in my life as those in Galatians 5. I'm guilty of so many of these—even if they're just thoughts I keep to myself. Cleanse my mind and help replace these bad habits with pure, good thoughts.

May I walk out your love and power as I serve your people—my husband, mom, siblings, family, friends, and coworkers. God, you are changing me here—taking away sinful habits and replacing them with your righteous qualities. I thought I came to Poland to make great money to have victory in our finances, but instead, I'm getting victory in many more parts of my life—over depression, over selfishness, over anger. Praise his goodness in my life!

Thank you for refining my heart and making it more like the person you know and see me be: rooted in my unchangeable identity of your favor.

Thank you for your grace and love when I mess up. Thank you for always being with me. Let me turn and praise you when I am getting angry. Let me have self-control. Ultimately let me be freed from my sins so I can show your love to others and do your will for me as part of your kingdom. In Jesus' name, I have all these glorious changes. Thank you, Lord!

"I am the true vine, and my Father is the gardener. He cuts off every branch in me that bears no fruit, while every branch that does bear fruit he prunes so that it will be even more fruitful. He cuts off every branch in me that bears no fruit, while every branch that does bear fruit he prunes so that it will be even more fruitful." John 15:1-2

Healthy roots were on the way as I made room for them to grow; pruning and tossing the sinful roots of weeds trying to choke my daily choice to walk in the Spirit. Every morning I would start my day by saturating my mind with God's Word. It became easier to recognize moments where I just needed to take a deep breath to rest and notice his love. I couldn't love others until I was choosing to be filled with God's love and truth.

As my perspective shifted from an aloof, unloving God to an intimate, compassionate Father, his Word became a treasured love letter for my heart. It came alive and spoke wisdom and comfort over me. As I felt safe to be loved and known, it was easier for me to let others know me and to give and receive love.

Even before my alarm, as the rising sun kissed the roofline of the city, I began waking up excited to dig into scripture and pray. God nourished my soul; his fullness and love strengthened me to fight against battles of my flesh. Each day through his mercies I could let go of yesterday's troubles and remember my sinful nature was crucified on the cross. I let go of the burden of my depression, shame, and past sins. The Lord freed me to receive his love and freely give it to others. Jesus says in the gospel of John:

> *"I am the vine; you are the branches. If you remain in me and I in you, you will bear much fruit; apart from me you can do nothing...If you keep my commands, you will remain in my love, just as I have kept my Father's commands and remain in his love. I have told you this so that my joy may be in you and that your joy may be complete. My command is this: Love each other as I have loved you."* John 15:5, 10-12

I saw immediate growth as I chose to abide with Jesus. I learned his heart and his voice. Joy and obedience came without striving as I prioritized my relationship with Jesus. Listening to him was easy because I understood him as a close friend. Peace flooded my heart, not because my friends changed, but because God changed me. As I had compassion for myself, it was easier to offer compassion for other people's struggles. My heart broke realizing many people may be suffering from beliefs rooted in lies and choking their ability to hope. God gave me more energy to love others and offer grace. Jesus was calling me to live through him, and his way of life is always one of sacrificial love.

This is how God showed his love among us: He sent his one and only Son into the world that we might live through him. This is love: not that we loved God, but that he loved us and sent his Son as an atoning sacrifice for our sins. Dear friends, since God so loved us, we also ought to love one another.
1 John 4:9-11

I learned truly loving others was a choice rather than a feeling. My feelings may change in a moment, but I can choose which of my thoughts I give time to. As I stood taller knowing my own identity, I was able to walk into a room and notice who needed love through an encouraging conversation. I made eye contact and smiled at strangers (which the Poles didn't always appreciate), but I ached for them to feel seen. I laid aside my old ways, my emotions, and insecurities, and decided to love. Would I love others even when it was inconvenient at best and painful at worst? Yes. *Love them as I love you, Sarah*, the Lord encouraged me.

We crossed a corroded, narrow steel bridge over a creek. Cobwebs and caked-on dirt obscured our sight. Down the embankment, we went looking for treasure for Katie. Locals on their Saturday morning stroll hurried by and tried not to make eye contact. I could not help but to inspect the connections, my engineering brain was curious.

I had never heard of geocaching until I met Katie, but it brought me joy seeing how she lit up explaining it to me. She loved the hunt, turning over rocks, checking between branches and crevices. If I didn't find the geocache, at least we were in nature on an adventure together. I loved spending time with Katie, whether we cooked together, went on walks, did our grocery shopping, or worked. We were practically inseparable. The Lord taught me how to love her and enjoy her companionship.

As I chose to abide in Jesus daily, my mind overflowed with a wellspring of gratitude understanding the simple gifts of life. I was filled with his Word and sought joy in every person and situation. I felt peace and deep love for others when I chose to act out of love. My brain eventually caught up with my actions. I put up a "no vacancy" sign in my mind for a self-centered and scarcity-minded worldview.

> *Finally, brothers and sisters, whatever is true, whatever is noble, whatever is right, whatever is pure, whatever is lovely, whatever is admirable—if anything is excellent or praiseworthy—think about such things. Whatever you have learned or received or heard from me, or seen in me—put into practice. And the God of peace will be with you.* Philippians 4:8-9

What a promise! The God of peace was alongside me as I set my mind on good things, giving people the benefit of the doubt and encouraging them.

> *The mind governed by the flesh is death, but the mind governed by the Spirit is life and peace.* Romans 8:6

I strolled along the Słupia River to join the church's out-reach ministry where ex-cons, recovering drug addicts, and cancer survivors shared testimonies of God's power and love in the park one warm Saturday afternoon. I took a meandering route to the gathering to support my friends. Praise bubbled up in my mind from a Psalm:

> *Blessed is the one who does not walk in step with the wicked*
> *or stand in the way that sinners take*
> *or sit in the company of mockers,*
> *but whose delight is in the law of the Lord,*
> *who meditates on his law day and night.*
> *That person is like a tree planted by streams of water,*
> *which yields its fruit in season and whose leaf*
> *does not wither—whatever they do prospers.*
> Psalm 1:1-3

My whole life was flourishing as my heart's roots spread in Jesus' love. I found joy meditating on his truth and applying it to my life. I soaked in his word and believed it to be true, then I was filled with hope and empowered to act on its wisdom.

Looking back at my life before Poland, I viewed myself as a neglected house plant stuck in a tiny pot without daily nourishment of God's love. The Lord lifted me up, shook me out, gave me fresh soil, and let me spread my root. He planted me in spacious soil of his goodness. I was never a trivial weed, but an ever-mightier oak, set among other beauties towering over me. God gave me my Polish community of believers to stand alongside me, rooted in truth, who reached out to me as they reached even higher for Jesus. I saw the good in their lives and desired that intimate, powerful relationship with the Lord too. The Holy Spirit encouraged us and empowered our minds to believe his promises as his children.

My branches reached for Jesus and my hope rose every week as the church shared more breakthroughs, healings, and miraculous provisions from our Father. I saw unwavering patience and hope. Pastors Marek and Ala waited five, ten, fifteen, twenty years, and beyond to see God fulfill his promises for their family and for the growth of the church. Through it all, they kept praising, kept praying, kept trusting God. I saw God's kingdom like the tiny mustard seed in one of Jesus' parables. The seed was planted in rich soil and God sent sunshine and rain. Eventually, the seed grew into a glorious tree. Its branches spread wide and birds rested in its shade.[20] Like trees sprouting from small seeds, we are intentionally designed to receive God's nourishment, as we wait for our season to flourish and offer blessings to others from our abundance.

In lush soil, God planted stories of hope. They encouraged me to continue to pursue him and expect good things to unfold in my life in his perfect timing. I began to see my Father's intentionally slow pace as the master gardener. I saw that faith is a walk, built on daily choices, to be nourished by reading the Bible, coming together in community, and heartfelt prayer and praise. Everything in life had a purpose. The more I embraced this and delighted in my daily life, the greater peace I found for my past, present, and future.

As Jesus said in John 15:5, apart from him I can do *nothing*. Sure, it once seemed like *"something"* in my eyes, but of lasting eternal impact? I had been missing out on the best, sweetest fruit. Good fruit takes time and work, but also a great deal of humility to trust him to do his part. Continually, I was reminded the Lord was working in the slow, hard seasons as his goodness sprung up around me in nature. Good fruit, like igniting hope in my community, is a natural result of being securely founded in Christ's love. Our relationship precedes our efforts, and when we're centered on that truth, joy, love, and peace are multiplied.

"But seek first his kingdom and righteousness, and all these things will be given to you as well."
Matthew 6:33

In Poland, as I began to grow and believe I was created for a unique godly purpose, new weeds were planted by the enemy. The seeds of doubt tried to choke my hope. How could I have a story to share? Who would listen? There were so many women with more impactful stories, more creative writing styles, more Instagram followers. There was no place for me to grow and flourish in this world. Those awful weeds of comparison and a scarcity mentality tried to stunt my growth. I believed all the spots were taken. I also feared I'd be drowned in the details—how could I share; how would I publish my story? How could I step forward without seeing the whole plan?

But God, in his abundance, wants to shower good gifts on all his children! He doesn't bathe all the trees in the forest with sunlight except me. How ridiculous! No, there will always be more than enough to nourish me. There is a place for me to stand and grow. There are people he has set in my path to nurture me with encouragement and love. He invites me to be steadfast and flourish where he planted me. When I get caught in the details of how and what this looks like, Jesus steps in, and asks me, like Peter, *"Do you love me? Then feed my sheep."*[21] It's simple: I get to love and share

Jesus in the unique way he created me to, in this moment and season. I get to grow in and reflect Jesus.

Uncomplicated, beautiful, Jesus.

I get to reach out and help those that desperately need to experience his love and tear out hope-choking lies. Jesus. I get to bring them Jesus.

After church one beautiful Sunday, I sat in the cafe of sunshine walls with a few friends. Leaves danced in the summer breezes outside the windows and dainty paper napkins marked our places as we sipped coffee and tea. Our conversation was light and enjoyable. Then suddenly, one friend, Damien, looked me dead in the eye, "You need to write a book, tell your story. Write about Poland. It'll be about 200 pages, take two years, and I'll help you with the distribution." I laughed awkwardly, "Sure, I do have a few good stories…" But something deep stirred in my heart. Then just before I left Poland, a beautiful godly woman at the church (who didn't speak any English), received a word from the Lord about me, "God has taught you so much here, and share it. Do not keep it to yourself," Gosia translated.

Months after I had returned home, God gave me a vision; it was how he saw me transformed and brought from death to life in Poland.

"As the rain and snow come down from heaven,
and do not return to it without watering the earth
and making it bud and flourish,

*so that it yields seed for the sower and bread for the
eater,
so is my word that goes out from my mouth:
it will not return to me empty, but will accomplish
what I desire and achieve the purpose for which I
sent it.
You will go out in joy and be led forth in peace;
the mountains and hills will burst into song before
you,
and all the trees of the field will clap their hands.
Instead of the thorn bush will grow the juniper,
and instead of briers, the myrtle will grow.
This will be for the Lord's renown, for an everlasting
sign,
that will endure forever."*
Isaiah 55:10-13

Did you catch those promises? His Word is never wasted
for me, for you, for all circumstances. This encouragement
was written to the Israelites, God's beloved people, after
they had been in exile and conquered by other rulers. God
spoke of hope and restoration for their families and generations to come. This message of hope still applies to us now.
Our loving Father cares for nations, peoples, families, and
for every individual to be rooted in his love and flourish.

Good fruit will come from what the Lord sews. It takes
time to bud. Sometimes it seems the rain will never fall
again. But he is faithful. Seeds of hope, his presence, and
love, that were planted in my heart as a young girl were
finally in full bloom.

You'll be led forth in joy and peace! Thorns of my past
were gone, God replaced them with beautiful, fruitful trees. I
didn't need to have my prickly defenses with Jesus. He knew

the shame and sin and chose to love me anyway. I could be vulnerable and did not need to hide my sin from him. God's desire was for me to repent, which is a biblical term meaning to turn from our old ways and return to God.[22] I realized my old thoughts and habits were broken, rotting roots and they kept me from flourishing. As such, I anticipated purposeful pruning so I would thrive. That is a life of sanctification from the wise Gardener with his children: to remove all things that hinder us from seeing his true heart and living out his best for us. And he continues to offer us a chance to return to his love.

"Those whom I love I rebuke and discipline. So be earnest and repent." Revelation 3:19

I see the beauty in the slowness of sowing, pruning, and reaping. I see the patient love of the Father sending his son Jesus over two thousand years ago, the Seed of Hope. He had me in mind as he wore his crown of thorns, carried my shame, and crucified my sins with him on the cross. Finally, he rose again, conquering death so I might have an abundant, fruitful life in him.

To God's glory, my life began flourishing in all areas—emotionally, physically, relationally, and spiritually. My new life is possible only because of the redemption story of Jesus. The truth of what has been done for me is unshakable. As a pine on the riverbanks in my childhood memories, I was finally growing strong roots, ever-reaching deeper into his love and truth.

Awakened by a New Economy

CHAPTER 12

Poles love to exercise and Biegam bo Lubię, BBL, translated "We Run Because We Love to" Club was no exception. People of all ages and abilities came together and created a beautiful community of runners, running just for the joy of it. The free running club met year-round and the organization had groups across Poland. Gosia was the insider who welcomed my coworkers and me into the local fabric of the community. We cheered for one other and they loved practicing their English with us. Sometimes we ran in my beloved forest, other times we did agility work on the track, sprinted across the grass barefoot, or had partner drills with medicine balls. "Kasia Fierce," aka Katie, my ever-dependable partner, would count our pass-crunches, "Jeden, dwa..." in her best Polish accent. The Poles applauded our willingness to work on our language skills as assimilating amerykański (Americans). We tried our best to understand the Polish instructions or looked to Gosia with pleading eyes for a quick translation.

Dew still glistened on the grass as I walked around the block, past my elderly neighbor friend, and up the hill to the Stadia—the local athletic facility and outdoor track. Plagued with "time optimism" I arrived late to the running club as they were several laps into their warm-up. BBL was our non-negotiable Saturday morning workout. "Hello, Sarah! How are you doing today?" Gosia practically sang jogging toward me. When I returned the question, matching her pace on the track, she predictably answered, "Fine, thank you!" with a giggle. She never had a complaint in the world. Two dozen people were scattered around the Stadia for warm-up laps before Coach Marcin started our dynamic stretches and drills.

My posse from work rapidly approached from behind. "Kasia Fierce," "Caramel Delight", and "Dapper" passed us at a good clip. "Hey, guys!" I hollered.

"Hey! It's 'Orlando's Bloom!'" Carmel Delight shouted back. Our nicknames were awarded by a group of peers. We gathered frequently at BBL, Aktywna Fabryka (Active Factory) for CrossFit, and Pole Fit. My buddies were regulars to the latter, but between you and me, I made a fully-clothed guest appearance and gave myself permission to laugh as I clung on for dear life and spun under the blacklights.

Honestly, did I love running? Not quite but an hour of exercise, encouraging friends, and endorphins always filled up my tank, rain or shine.

After running club, I would usually make breakfast and sit on my balcony, soaking in the rays. Sometimes I would read, other times I'd sit quietly in the late morning, watching the bustling city beyond.

Living in Poland brought a new stillness to my life. I had always lived with somebody: family, roommates, or Andrés. Whenever I came home, everything was always exactly how I left it and it was quiet. Although I was alone in my flat, I never turned on the TV or streamed Netflix from my laptop. I found better things to do. I moved to Poland with three suitcases and a backpack—not even enough to fill my bedroom's wardrobe. I had more than I needed: another bedroom, living/dining/kitchen space, and a bathroom big enough to park a Fiat. Having this much living space is atypical in Poland. My life was much simpler than back home; I had less to wash, clean, and organize. Other than a few small stacks of books here and there, the tops of my tables and furniture were bare. Though my flat was fairly empty, I didn't miss the decorations and knick-knacks I had in the States. I found rest in my new home.

Local restaurants were inexpensive and delicious, but I typically tried to save money and cook for myself and my friends. I had a tiny oven that was barely two feet wide, but enough to roast veggies for guests. At least twice a week, I went to the local grocery store, Biedronka, with the giant ladybug logo. My small haul was divided between my two mini-fridges. Thankfully, Biedronka was a short walk, or just one round-about away from home by car.

Adventures of shopping included: learning to read ingredients to ensure they adhered to my Whole 30 paleo diet with Katie, trying the numerous herbal teas and European chocolates, and mastering the crazy coinage of the Polish Złoty currency. In the beginning, the poor cashier didn't have much patience as a trail of stern customers piled up behind me. Frozen with anxiety, I tried to process her stream of unrecognizable syllables, but my mind went dark. Reaching into my wallet, the clink of the coins fell in my hand and she deftly selected the right combination. *Next time*, I thought, *I'll pay with my debit card.*

Did I mention I had my own washer and dryer? The dryer's heating technology was different from what I was used to in the States and it took three hours to complete a load. I tried the local method: a drying rack. It fit in my expansive bathroom and I felt good about saving energy. I loved my routines, and every Saturday I'd clean my apartment from top to bottom—laundry, dusting, vacuuming, mopping, scrubbing. (Well, if you ask Andrés, he'll tell you I've always loved to clean. It's true, I did come from a long line of tidy English women). I was recharged as I cleaned and listened to worship music or podcasts.

Chores and other daily tasks weren't a burden, I knew I had time to do them well. I made space for these weekly rhythms in my life. My goal was to have an orderly home for Sunday, my day to recharge and focus on relationships with friends, and most importantly, Jesus.

The whisper of the Holy Spirit, the still, small voice invited me to come into his rest.

Before Poland, God was patient with me, even as I had rushed around like the Road Runner with a cloud of dust left in my wake. When I took the time to rest in the Lord, pray, and sense his Spirit I felt his love, peace, and gentle correction. I was strengthened in him, not weakened or ashamed. I often believed I needed to earn love and value from others and God. On days I'd try to rest, I'd get anxious and frustrated and after a few hours of Netflix, I'd turn into a cleaning monster and taskmaster. Andrés would be cozy on the couch, annoyed and dumbfounded I couldn't be still.

My soul needed rest, not cheap entertainment or distractions that filled my brain with junk. I ached for stillness but didn't know how to get it.

I didn't want to continue to be anxious and constantly moving but I didn't know how to change. My schedule was loaded down with professional society activities, meetings, work mixers, church bell choir (my great grandfather was also a bellringer) and committees, Bible study, and service projects. These things were all good things, but they kept me busy, even overwhelming me at times. Who suffered? I did. My marriage. My friendships. But especially my relationship with Jesus. I didn't make time to invest in intentional relationships. Andrés lovingly supported my over-achieving, people-pleaser schedule, but he took the brunt of my impatience, stress, and unpredictable outbursts. No wonder I was miserable. Those outward sins reflected the health of my heart and the wrong beliefs I had about rest.

My poor, exhausted soul. I was striving and getting crushed by burdens I was compelled to carry alone.

But there is a different way for us to live!

Jesus beckons to you and me,

"Come to me, all you who are weary and burdened, and I will give you rest. Take my yoke upon you and learn from me, for I am gentle and humble in heart, and you will find rest for your souls. For my yoke is easy and my burden is light." Matthew 11:28-30

It reminds me of a moment at the beach recently. My sweet Annabelle, less than two, collected her beloved rocks at the beach. As her sandy hands clutched several stones to her

145

chest, she was determined to grab one more rock. Bending down, a wave surprised her, and all her precious stones tumbled into the surf. "Uh oh!" I comforted her, "It's ok, little Bug."

God spoke to my heart, "Sarah, were you not once just like that, my precious daughter?" I can see the struggle I had trying to carry everything myself. Now I see God's patience waiting for me to *choose to release* the burdens, asking for my Father's help. He will do the heavy lifting. Poland was a beautiful start to my new rhythm of release and rest.

> *The Lord is my shepherd, I lack nothing.*
> *He makes me lie down in green pastures,*
> *he leads me beside quiet waters,*
> *he refreshes my soul.*
> *He guides me along the right paths*
> *for his name's sake.*
> Psalm 23:1-3

I was not meant to wander, carrying the stones of life on my own. The Lord invited me to surrender to his rest and trust in his path of peace for my life. I found his rest in Poland.

Finally, I felt like a sweet, peaceful sheep sitting in a lush green field. His presence was all around me.

God began giving me discernment to pursue his best for my life. His best meant saying no to distractions, especially on Sundays. I didn't play catch up and knock out my to-do list. It was just Jesus and Sabbath resting: Community, being together, free of anxiety, slow-paced, family time, strolls in the forest, quietly reading on a park bench by the pond, no social media, or emails. Many local stores were closed in downtown Słupsk, reinforcing my new rhythm. I trusted God to make time for work and responsibilities outside of Sunday. He honored my heart's desires. On Mondays, I woke up excited for the week, refreshed. My spirit had been recharged being with Jesus and taking his easy path. I let go of my burdens and was amazed at the Lord's power and provision. He was always moving and working in my circumstances, on my behalf, refining my heart. I received his grace and gave myself space to just be.

My new pace of life was modeled in my Polish church—it was intimate and simple. Come to worship and pray on Thursdays and Sundays. They welcomed everyone, and the members and staff were approachable despite occasional language barriers. The church wasn't bogged down with endless meetings or causes. Their heart was to share Jesus' love to the broken and lost and be open to the Spirit's leading. Fruits of joy, peace, abundance, and humility were overflowing. I saw the members walking out the gospel in all aspects of their lives. They didn't have life in tidy boxes of secular and non-secular work. Jesus' love and power were woven through it all, every day. It was a beautiful rhythm of grace. Financial problems? Pray. Common colds? Pray. Tough decisions at work? Pray. Faith was in action through their entire life as we trusted God's promises to provide.

Wait, can you hold on a sec, I need to post this on Insta... never came out of my mouth in Poland, and from May to July I fasted from all social media. I didn't have a cell phone connected to a network, meaning I had to live at the mercy of Wi-Fi. My work phone was one of those burner types spies use with basic capabilities for calls and texts, except mine was neon red. Life in the wild without a smartphone turned out to be one of the biggest blessings for building community. When I was out of my house, I couldn't be buried in my phone—my apps didn't work, it was futile! Instead, I looked friends in the eye and got lost in laughter and good conversations over milkshakes, burgers "bez bułki" (without a bun), and onion rings. I hiked trails through pine trees to desolate dunes, pristine beaches, and strolled through the city. I delighted in simple wonders like songbirds, expressions of strangers waiting for buses, and noticed how people decorated their windows. I was present and enjoyed the presence of others. My soul was satisfied. I still crave to create that deep level of connection for the rest of my life. Don't you long for something like that, friend?

In the stillness of my new rhythm, the Lord spoke to me. He had always been speaking, but I had been too hurried to listen. His presence captivated me—whether in the forest by myself or with my dear friends. I felt his love and knew he was calling me to enjoy the day he had laid before me. Numbing with entertainment or cheap thrills of "likes" on social media posts lost their appeal. Joy sprung up as I invested in relationships and asked good questions. I let myself daydream as I drank in all the beauty around me. My wayfarer heart led me through the city with eyes wide to notice the needs of others and pray. I prayed for what I saw, sensed, and for people and situations that popped up from memory.

I went to Poland knowing I would only be there for a short while, but I made a deliberate choice to engage with the community. I made friends at work and church. Then, to my surprise, my church friends became friends with my work friends. God gave me a beautiful blend of friendship with everyone I knew in Słupsk. At work, they knew I loved

Jesus, and at church, they knew I had a high-demand job, but good company on base. I felt no shame for who I was and didn't compartmentalize the sacred and secular. All aspects gracefully wove together as I saw God in all of it. God used me as a link to unite my American coworkers with my loving church community.

Even now in 2020, Americans still attend their church services. Gosia excellently translates her father's messages to English on the stage of their new church's auditorium. The church opened its new doors in the spring of 2020. Much construction still needs to be completed, but they gather each week on Gorgotta Street in the partially revived hangar and continue to pray in agreement with the Lord's provision and perfect timing.

Do you feel anxious to always hustle and strive for more? Do you give in to the pressure from popular culture telling us there's only a tiny window to share what we have, otherwise someone else will steal our opportunity? My mindset shifted in Poland; I was not designed to work tirelessly seven days a week, which was divergent from my upbringing in American culture. I was awakened by God's economy. It was far greater than anything I had ever imagined—boundless storehouses for his beloved daughter. I was done striving in my own strength, apart from Jesus. My efforts had left me exhausted, overwhelmed, and unfruitful.

Jesus' ways were better. *Come abide in my love*, he called from his lush pasture. *Rest in me and let me multiply your work. Trust in me in the waiting, let go of your burdens. Seasons of growth and harvest will come in my time.*

Reflecting on my time in Poland, God showed me how he worked as I slowed to his intentional pace. I learned he could use all aspects of my life to love people. I didn't need to leave Jesus in a tidy box for Sundays. The Holy Spirit was able to love through me as I listened and encouraged coworkers. Jesus knew my heart and personality—I didn't need to directly evangelize coworkers, but I was prayerful and intentional with my responses. Most importantly, I was transformed by God's love and realized it wasn't about my efforts or limited capacity—it was about his overwhelming love and storehouses of blessings for all his children.

Can I love people? Absolutely, as I abide in Jesus' love and make space for him to multiply his grace.

August 2016
Spilsby, England

Royal Blood

CHAPTER 13

S trands of fake pearls, polyester dresses, and musty fur hats were strewn across the yard with my siblings. We were invited to a royal wedding and had to prepare for such a grand event.

Snap! My mom took a photo capturing us with the neighborhood kids parading down the sidewalk aisle covered in dandelions. I made a fantastic mother of the bride.

As a little girl, I believed I was worth knowing, I just wasn't known yet. I had this hope in my heart I was part of the royal family. Evidence confirmed it. Mom was born in England and Grammie still had a proper English accent. Grammie discussed the Queen and her family with such intimacy that we just *had* to be related, I reasoned with myself. I burst with pride in my British roots and thought I was special and better than my commoner American classmates and friends. I believed my family was wealthy based on my grandparents' three-bedroom ranch with a few acres, screen house, tire swing, and bottomless cookies in a yellow smiley-face jar.

I don't recall the exact moment when I realized Grammie wasn't of royal lineage. Perhaps I was 11 or 12, just as I was

151

developing into a young lady and studying my family tree for a school assignment.

Devastated.

In my young mind, this was quite a blow to my fantasy. To be American felt so lack-luster.

My siblings, mom, and other family members had flown across the pond to visit our family, especially my great grandmother, Beatrice. She passed away on my 17th birthday, only weeks before her 91st. Great Gram was one for a laugh and never took things too seriously. She once told me she hated school and it was OK if I didn't like it either. Legally blind, but when she looked me in the eyes, I knew she really saw me.

Cousin Charlie was also a favorite of mine, who met me just before I turned two. A contemplative and happy man, and a "lorry driver" by trade in England.

Everyone would recount the wonders of England: steaming hot fish and chips wrapped in newspaper, enchanted sweet shops, tiny homes, winding brick paths in the blossoming gardens, and refreshing rain showers. I treasured gifts from England—a necklace from my mom on my 11th birthday, postcards of magical castles and lands explored, and lots of candy. The aroma of Jelly Bellies and Cadbury Smarties still lingers in my memory.

"Pack a nice dress," Grammie encouraged just days before my departure. "I have a little surprise for us!" In the late summer of 2016, I finally visited the place of wonder that had culminated since my earliest memories.

I took a selfie at the airport, then I boarded the Wizz Air flight with Katie's loaner hiking backpack. I was off on an adventure and my trip even aligned with Grammie's "holiday" (vacation). I stayed with her childhood best friend, Ann, a peaceful, warmhearted widow living in a small town where these ladies met more than three-quarters of a century ago. The morning after I arrived, I woke up with stillness in my soul; birds chirped in the garden outside my window.

My heart swelled as I stepped into family history. I stood in the stone church where my mom was christened and the same church where my grandparents wed. As Grammie and I strolled in the cool of the morning, she recalled living just down the lane from her grandparents and where she used to play between the brick row homes. I sat on the bench where the town phone once resided. Where, more than 60 years ago, Grammie sat in the evenings to call her betrothed American, at the Air Base in East Kirby. I walked through the local cemetery and paused as Grammie cleaned the graves of our loved ones.

The people and places woven into my family history were coming to life: the petrol station where Grammie had her first job, the rolling hills, and double-decker buses. My heart delighted in the landscape. The countryside was dotted with quaint farms, cozy brick homes, and well-manicured hedges. Dew clung to the grass and dazzled in the rising rays on my morning jogs.

The day after I arrived, I stepped into a childhood dream. In my black-and-white A-line dress and a gray "cardi," I followed Grammie, Ann, and Val to our special surprise. We arrived at a beautiful bed and breakfast just outside the village. High ceilings held shimmering chandeliers and dainty floral decor set the elegant tone. Fine china graced our table with trays of delicate sandwiches, treats, and bottomless cups of black tea. Using my best etiquette and poise,

I squared my shoulders, nibbled treats, and sipped tea. I was a princess at high tea after all.

Despite the beauty around me, I felt burdened in my spirit. I needed to breathe. I needed my spirit refilled. I sensed a heaviness over the land and especially in my family tree. There were deep unspoken undercurrents. But God was revealing his hope of restoration for my family. He nudged me, "Don't dwell on the past, I have come that they may have a life to the full, to release prisoners from captivity. Bring light into the darkness."

I discerned my family had raw stories and painful memories, but we didn't openly speak about them. It grieved me to feel the weight and quiet suffering. More importantly, I yearned for them to know there was still hope! I desperately wanted them to experience the hope and love I found in Jesus. Restoration. Healing. Forgiveness. Freedom, sweet freedom. I too once felt hopelessly lost.

But Jesus spoke hope.

Jesus answered them, "It is not the healthy who need a doctor, but the sick. I have not come to call the righteous, but the sinners to repentance." Luke 5:31-32

Just before my English caper ended, Grammie, Val, Charlie, and I went to the seaside to have a stroll with our "99's" (soft-serve ice cream). With sand squishing between my toes, I was no longer a toddler, but Charlie still delighted in me. He stooped down, picking up a rock, and handed it to me. "This is for you, Sarah. It's a heart." *Oh, my heart.*

I know there is hope for deeper restoration for my family, I had experienced it personally, but at the time I didn't know what to say. I only did what I knew I could; I quietly prayed, expressed how much I love them, and shared how God healed me from depression as we waited at the airport sipping tea from travel cups.

I boarded the plane after kissing Charlie, Val, and especially Grammie. I sighed, exhausted, "Lord, my family is in your hands."

I am expectant of God to work the seeds into the ground. May my own pain and story bring light to the cultivation of a life lived in God's truth. I ache for them to experience the freedom that comes from releasing our pasts and embracing the hope and love Jesus offers.

Letting go of earthly hope in my English heritage, I embrace the unshakable royalty Jesus gives. My crown is never tarnished. My dress is without blemish or wrinkle, it's not from my dress-up box of hand-me-downs. It's tailored especially for me; regal and beautiful.

I am a daughter of the King and I pray my family would join me and receive this beautiful, adopted bloodline. No one is too far from the love of Jesus. *Lord, soften their hearts. You love them even more than I could imagine.*

I see the brokenness of where I came from and what dwells in me. I see roots of pain and sorrow, trying to keep me small and hopeless. The enemy of my soul whispers lies from the same old record—*see all this ugliness! God can't use you. You're broken. You're nobody. No royal bloodline.* Lies. No Satan! I will not accept these ideas. The conniving wolf constantly threshes lies over the truth. Over time, my discernment has grown even as I heard the same scratchy record play. I am redeemed and God's rebuilding and renewing things that have been devastated for generations. The broken patterns of the past are destroyed. Jesus is reviving this bloodline because of his goodness, and I am part of this transformation!

Soon after visiting my relatives in England, I remember Gosia summarizing it perfectly, "Sarah, your family is your mission field." My heart burned and tears welled in my eyes. I felt this was true, now that my spiritual life had grown to a healthy place God was calling my attention outward instead of inward. I can now see slow fruit emerging from many prayers and hopes. Just as I saw Jesus work miracles with Andrés, and later with my sister's brisk north-Atlantic baptism, I see God's rays of hope breaking through the clouds. One brother even asked me to read a draft of this book.

I continue to love and pray for my family, but I cannot let the weight render me ineffective. Jesus doesn't intend for me to fix my family. It is Christ who does the work, but I do get to have a front seat to the redemption stories unfolding, my own story as a testament. I have the mind of Christ. He has freed me from these negative thought patterns and self-sabotaging behaviors.

They will rebuild ancient ruins and restore places long devastated; they will renew ruined cities that have been devastated for generations. Isaiah 61:4

The new legacy of my family is being written; a new, eternal regalness surrounds me. And I expectantly wait for my Father to unfold his redemption for my family and the generations to come to be part of his unshakeable kingdom.

Great Grammie and me when I was ten.

More than Conquerors

CHAPTER 14

Darkness before my dawn

Alone. Dark. Gasping for air. Walls surrounded me; I was held captive between a gripping fear of dying and wanting everything to fade to black.

I gave my heart to Jesus as a child, earnestly praying in the quiet of the night.

But twenty years later, I still was tormented, stuck in the darkness of depression, believing no one understood my suffering. Not even Jesus. No relief, no hope, no joy was possible. New life was available to me, but I didn't know I had received it as I prayed in my bunk bed with the octagon window looking out to the pines.

A loud voice cut through my lies, "Little girl, I say to you, get up!"

I was never meant to stay in my grave, hopeless, helpless, and unloved.

Arise, sweet Sarah, you are free. The power of death holds nothing over you. Your life is not dead, it is not without hope. Now rise up, awake, dear Sarah. Resurrected Jesus resurrects my life.

Light cut through the darkness; chains of sin and shame were shattered. And I arose. "W imię Jezusa!" (In the name of Jesus!)

Jesus reached out and offered his power to dwell in me, released from captivity. Do I believe it? Yes, Lord Jesus. I am ready for you to revive my heart. Breathe your life into my lungs.

I was set free in May of 2016 because Jesus conquered first. He suffered for all my sins and shame, nailing them to the cross, and burying them in the tomb. Gone. Done. Once for all. I have new life.

The enemy told me for too long because of my past, I was worthless, powerless, hopeless. Ultimately, I was trapped believing a false gospel that my life was beyond the reach of Jesus' restoration. But no! Those suffocating lies finally were buried where they ought to be: the grave.

My healer, Jesus, the resurrector of life, met me. He called me by name and gave me a new life.

Even death was not strong enough to separate his love for me. He is the Risen King, fighting battles for me, bringing my heart to the Father, ceaselessly interceding on my behalf.

As Romans says:

Who then condemns? No one. Christ Jesus who died—more than that, who was raised to life—is at the right hand of God and is also interceding for us. Who shall separate us from the love of Christ? Shall trouble or hardship or persecution or famine or nakedness or danger or sword? As it is written: 'For your sake, we face death all day long; we are considered as sheep to be slaughtered.' No, in all these things we are more than conquerors through him who loved us. Romans 8:34-37

Jesus stepped out of the grave and called me out of my own. My hope is alive! Death could not keep Jesus' love from saving me. Joyful, abundant life starts now as I run to my Jesus in awe of his majesty. He pulls me in close and whispers to me:

I have great things for you, my beloved, Jesus assures me. *I use the weak and foolish to confuse the wise. I have created you and your story, your heartbreaks, and dreams, exactly as I intended. Nothing will be wasted. Just keep walking in my Spirit. Abide. Spread your roots and let them draw from the cease-less springs of my living water. Prepare to be amazed by the mountains I will move.*

After Jesus rose from the dead and the Holy Spirit was released to his people, we were given the resurrection power of Christ to abide in us. Since the garden of Eden, God's plan was always to dwell with his people. He has always wanted intimacy with us. He is not a distant, angry God judging from afar. No. On the contrary, he wants to walk with us, as we walk with him, together in the cool of the garden.

He knows my frail heart. I am a sinner by nature.

For he knows how we are formed,
he remembers that we are dust.
Psalm 103:14

By God bringing me into a healthier place, I was able to look at both the truth of my story and the truth of God and finally be free. I found my voice. God moved mountains in my life and in the community around me. Freedom radiated from me when I stood on his truth and walked out the power of the gospel. I was forgiven. Loved. Chosen. Adopted. My spirit is seated with Christ in heavenly places.

I am enough because Jesus is. Surrendering my hopes, my dreams, my shame, and my sins. I am free to love, be loved, and share my story of transformation because Jesus conquered for me.

Can I get a hallelujah? We don't have to measure up! Christ did it for me. He did it for you, too, sweet friend.

I knew in my heart my ugliest sins were forgiven and I was free. Jesus came so I "may have life, and have it to the full."[23] I found my life when I experienced the power in Jesus' love in action through his miracles, encouragement, and his people in Poland. I saw others walking boldly in their identity, radically healed by his love. Cancers and heart conditions healed without medical treatment, financial blessings beyond human reasoning, unbridled joy, and zest for life. I saw Jesus, alive, and moving in the small and big things alike. He was in all of it and I wanted to take a front seat to his work.

I had lived too long allowing my feelings and other people to influence my identity and calling. I longed for a fulfilling life, but it kept falling flat without inviting God's power to work through me. Playing whack-a-mole with circumstances held me captive. This is the last "mole", then I can have joy. Ok, one more trial, and then I can have peace. It was futile.

But Jesus wanted me to invite him into my daily battles and let him rewrite my old narrative. He challenged me to rejoice in trials, because he was still with me, loving me, strengthening me, and sanctifying me. I wasn't meant to fix myself. Instead, I was meant to rest in his power and delight in him. The more time I spent with him, the more I got to shine his love and light for others and give him space to work in my heart.

Now I look at my past and see his faithfulness. I can honestly say my suffering has brought me deeper into his love and for that alone—I am grateful for the pain. He conquered and redeemed my depression and shame. I continually experience the power of his love as he restores my life. He's given me a freedom song.

Like a city on a hill, Jesus set me ablaze; loved and restored by his power. For too long, the deceiver twisted my story to convince me it was powerless. But really, he was shaking in his boots, knowing the power of my true voice in Christ.

I am more than a conqueror!

Now I walk unashamed of who I am because of whose I am.

I want to get my hopes up in the God of miracles every day! This has become one of my favorite verses to declare over my life, especially when I am discouraged:

> *May the God of hope fill you with all joy and peace as you trust in him so that you may overflow with hope by the power of the Holy Spirit.* Romans 15:13

I claim it for me now. I claim it for *you*! God is still working; his Spirit is alive and active. His presence surrounds me. He's not finished with me; I have a calling on my life. It was a calling beyond what my 28-year-old mind could fathom. A calling beyond my engineering career, beyond my family, beyond what I had ever believed possible. I am in awe of God's loving hand on my life, leading me to higher grounds and unimaginable freedom.

Abundant life with Jesus starts now. You can have it too, friend. Give your heart to the lover of your soul. Walk out of your grave and into your true identity as his beloved. Walk into freedom. Be filled with his love and give hope to others. Claim his strength and worthiness as yours. He wants to speak to your heart today.

Know I have struggled with how hard this is to grasp. Know God works patiently with us, if this still seems like miles away from where your heart is now, God is waiting, and will never give up on you.

On my last Sunday in Słupsk, I strolled past my favorite cracked building, along the Słupia River, through the park, and over the cobble path with my tea travel mug, journal, and Bible. My heart was heavy knowing I would leave this beautiful place in a few short days. Autumn leaves crunched under my feet and trees stood bare once again.

Welcomed in the lobby of the church, I was home. The service began with a joyous chorus of Polish syllables. I sang at the top of my lungs, arms raised, as tears streamed down. Although I had learned much of the language, my spirit knew the words beyond my comprehension. After Pastor Marek's message, I rose to receive a special blessing from him, Ala, and the church. I thanked them for their love and community. I promised, "I will not forget what God has done here. Although my heart breaks to leave you, I know we'll be together again, in eternity praising our loving Father together… in Polish of course!" And I truly meant it, wiping back joyful tears, looking into their loving eyes. I had tangible, palpable hope. Jesus captured my heart in Poland and surrounded me with his beautiful presence.

And now I continue to pray and fan the flame inside me:

Father, I desperately want a meaningful connection with you and to share your beautiful presence and the power it unleashes to change lives. I want to run hard after you and let my heart overflow with joy knowing your purposes will be accomplished, and we have the promise of your presence through it all. The pain from this life will not be wasted, but instead, be redeemed for your honor and glory. The purpose of my relationship with you is to know your love intimately and be transformed into Christ's likeness.

165

And so I hold onto Paul's encouragement to the Corinthians.

Therefore we do not lose heart. Though outwardly we are wasting away, yet inwardly we are being renewed day by day. For our light and momentary troubles are achieving for us an eternal glory that far outweighs them all. So we fix our eyes not on what is seen, but on what is unseen, for what is seen is temporary, but what is unseen is eternal.
2 Corinthians 4:16-18

Jesus.
I will keep my eyes fixed on Jesus.

Gosia and me after the closing worship set at a conference
on invincibility in Christ. My heart was bursting
with joy for Jesus and love for my sweet friend.

November 2016
Słupsk, Poland

The (Un)surprise Party

CHAPTER 15

I rolled over in my cozy bed with the square pillow and matching comforter sans top sheet to turn off the alarm. Opening the shades, the cool light of dawn filled the room. Smoke sleepily rose from chimneys and the cityscape of red roofs had a whisper of white. Winter was coming, in Poland and in my heart. In a few days, I would be leaving my beautiful Polish home.

The experiences and insights the Lord planted in me were going to be covered by the comfort and protection of his Holy Spirit. He would work deep below the surface into the roots of my heart. He was preparing me for new things, but first I needed the approaching hard season to solidify and strengthen what he taught me. He knew the pain of my new winter would draw me forward to spring as I chose to continue to walk in obedience and seek him in trials. But at the time, I couldn't see the goodness of it. I believed my life back in the States would continue in perpetual flourishing, but deep inside I felt changes were coming. I always disliked disruptions to good things, and I had found myself in Poland. I feared I wouldn't be the same person back home. Or worse, I would fall back into depression and be captive to my spiraling thoughts and lose the ability to sense the closeness of the Lord.

As Ecclesiastes says:

There is a time for everything, and a season for every activity under the heavens:
A time to be born and a time to die,
A time to plant and a time to uproot,
A time to kill and a time to heal,
A time to tear down and a time to build,
A time to weep and a time to laugh,
A time to mourn and a time to dance,
A time to scatter stones and a time to gather them,
A time to embrace and a time to refrain from embracing,
A time to search and a time to give up,
A time to keep and a time to throw away,
A time to tear and a time to mend,
A time to be silent and a time to speak,
A time to love and a time to hate,
A time for war and a time for peace...
He has made everything beautiful in its time. He has also set eternity in the human heart; yet no one can fathom what God has done from beginning to end.
Ecclesiastes 3:1-8,11

Fighting the onset of winter, I relished my summer and fall. I saw joy, hope, and love overflowing in my heart. I saw my inner beauty. Salty cries washed away the pain and shame I had carried for decades. I gave myself space to grieve the loss of my childhood innocence. I rejoiced with tears knowing I had new hope to move forward; I had hope because I was truly loved and known by Jesus. I was no longer paralyzed by my past and terrified for my future.

Long Polish days were gone and evening came abruptly. I lit candles to unwind, listened to worship music and sobbed. My heart was exploding feeling the depth of Jesus' love for me. He comforted me with the lyrics from "Because of Your Love."[24] It was a song for my story—one about the fierce pursuit of my Father with his tenderhearted whispers of love. The weight of the work he had done in my heart over eight short months shook me to the core. And all I could do was weep in appreciation and feel a calm assurance my life would never be the same.

God had one more love letter for me, my last week in Słupsk. It was an unsuspecting Monday. At work, I had my routine breakfast with Katie of medium-boiled eggs and bananas with almond butter as we overlooked the frosted field. *Snap.* A picture memorialized our routine meal, holding hands over our treasured, imported butter.

Despite spitting rain and wind biting my cheeks, I completed my prayer lap around the runway on base. The new buildings arose around me and construction went on as usual. I played a part in laying these new foundations. Within myself, I felt the Lord affirm the work he had laid in my heart for his good purposes. I don't recall what I prayed, but I walked with intention and spoke with conviction.

The day rolled into the evening; it was Bible study night. The usual ladies were Ala, Gosia, Justyna, Joanna,

Loretta, and me. But surprisingly Katie asked to join. "Of course!" I exclaimed.

Katie and I had dinner at the et Cetera with a coworker and his family. "Dapper" stopped by to pick up takeout, waved, and hurried along. We finished our meal and then went on our way to Filmowa Street.

But then Katie received a suspicious call from "Caramel Delight" as we got into the car. I could clearly hear him "Do you have the package?... We're ready!" and deduced they were scheming a gathering. Sure enough, after climbing four flights of stairs, down the sunny yellow hall and past the foyer full of jackets— "SURPRISE!" The whole sanctuary was bursting with smiling faces, all there for me—coworkers and their spouses and my church family. Gosia said I didn't look surprised and I should have tried. But well-pleased, a smile slipped across my face. I held up my Bible and Beth Moore *Breaking Free* study guide, "Ok, who's ready to dig in?!" I was only half-joking.

We filed into the cafe with a parade of laughter and dug into the beautiful spread. Plenty of Polish goodies including goose pierogi from the et Cetera (thanks, "Dapper") were served with salads, sweets, and a farewell cake. I lingered at each table, soaking in the conversation. I treasured each person, and I could feel their love emanate in reminiscent stories and long embraces. "Carmel Delight" had a small speech. Katie and I cried and clung to one another. "Success!" He exclaimed with his infectious giggle, "I wanted to see the waterworks!"

I learned three things that evening:

1. I am still terrible with surprises. Ask Andrés about all the ruined secrets since we've dated. I'm a super sleuth without trying.

2. People *actually* love me as I am, not as I'm trying to be someone else or please anyone, but inherently just as God created me. I had only been in Słupsk for eight months but had deep, meaningful relationships.

3. God delights in me! He actually, truly, really loves *me*. Intensely. Perfectly.

I struggled to say goodbye to my dear friends, friends who knew me and saw me blossom. Perhaps "Orlando's Bloom" was a more fitting nickname than I could have ever imagined. My heart was overwhelmed by their genuine love and appreciation for me. I felt treasured and accepted.

The Lord stirred my heart and the room's buzz of conversation and laughter faded away, *This is only a glimpse of how much I love you, my daughter.*

I was surprised after all but in such a deeper, lasting sense. I was restored by the power of Jesus' love. He chased me to foreign lands, wooed me into his presence, built my trust, healed my wounds, and set me free. I chose to walk boldly knowing who I am and whose I am. My heart learned to beat in sync with his love. I felt fulfilled, known, and deeply loved.

I don't have to be anyone else but myself. I am a unique, beautiful expression of Jesus' love.

I am loved exactly as I am.
I have a story. And it's the story of love:
I am loved.
And I love you, my Jesus.

Winter 2020
San Luis Obispo, California

Hope Rises from Winter

EPILOGUE

Winter in San Luis Obispo reminds me of late spring in Poland. Drenching rains satisfied the parched Earth, and tiny shoots sprouted along my favorite hiking trails. It's my favorite season in "SLO" as the locals call it, because of the magnificent shades of green and cleansing rains. Hope rises from what seems dry and dead. I drank in the smell of fresh air, wild sage, and ocean breezes.

The beautiful seeds the Lord planted in my heart more than three years ago were faithfully coming to life.

My winter seasons leading into spring in California were dark and lonely. I left Poland in November of 2016 and returned to Massachusetts. My heart ached to feel the peace and rest of Jesus' presence; my solid foundation seemed to crumble beneath me. I lost my community, my church, my joy, my Poland. As if a faucet had been turned off, my inner peace and joy were gone. How could I be in such a hard place after walking so closely with Jesus? I kept reading the Word, kept praying, but I felt numb. God was quiet. Did I do something wrong?

My heart felt chained in Massachusetts. Overwhelm became my predominant emotion with every task and responsibility: work, exercise, sitting in traffic through the wintry mix, grocery shopping at Market Basket with every other New Englander wearing miserable faces, going to church, and small talk with the parishioners. At least once a week, I'd sob in a ball on my couch because I didn't feel God's presence anymore. Everything seemed dead. Poor Andrés didn't know how to console me. He couldn't grasp the deep work the Lord had done in my heart. Between tears, I said, "I want to go home." Confused and hurt he said, "But you *are* home."

In the silence, I wrestled with my feelings and memories. I yearned for what I had in Słupsk. I doubted God could ever do anything more loving or miraculous for me. My best life was over at 28. My friend Loretta had given me a farewell present including a beautiful letter affirming the calling God gave me, and Joyce Meyer's devotional, *Battlefield of the Mind*. But when I received it, I confidently thought it was wonderful, but I wouldn't need the book. I had already been set free from my depression, anxiety, and poor thought life. Little did I know it would be the life support to help me limp along in the dark valleys.

My poor impressionable heart was entangled in lies, not hoping for new, good things, not fixing my eyes on the God of hope.

Iulia and I had a sleepover only weeks after my homecoming in late November. She had moved a few states away while I was abroad but came to visit for the holidays. That evening, Iulita interrupted me as I cleaned up our dinner dishes in my dated 90's oak kitchen. Hugging me, she looked into my eyes, and said, "You are so beautiful." I felt like a mess: wet hair, bathrobe, and dark circles from a never-ending workweek. I longed for the wholeness in my heart I had in Poland. I wanted purpose. I wanted hope. I didn't feel beautiful. I felt empty, frustrated, and afraid I'd never feel God's love ever again. The sly enemy convinced me to live in shame and suffer quietly with these thoughts. Unfortunately, I went back to old comfortable habits of closing people off, even Iulia, who knew my whole life story—the good, bad, and ugly, and loved me anyway.

I tried to find the next international adventure to lift my spirits. Three weeks in Chennai, India materialized to support my team on a different aspect of the Poland project. New hope rose. I got vaccinated, completed visa applications, but never booked my ticket. My role was cut. Completely deflated, I wallowed in disappointment unsure of God's next big move for me.

Now I see my walk of faith will change as seasons do, but God still loves me through it all. Since returning from Poland, God did not stop speaking or loving me. However, he waited for me in the stillness. Back in my "normal" rhythm of life, busyness shouted louder than his unimposing voice of love. After three months at home, I was in Washington D.C. alone in the quietness of my hotel room. I shut out distractions and calmed my anxious mind. His presence refreshed my spirit like a nomad finding a cool drink in a barren desert. Morning shone through the sheer drapes; the Lord hadn't left me! But the moment didn't last.

During the same time, Andrés was offered a work reloca-
tion to California. I didn't love Massachusetts, but I didn't
love the Golden State either. It felt like I was getting pulled
further from where and who I was in Poland. I doubted my
transformation, did I really change in Poland? Did I make
it up? Am I really loved? I got lost in a torrent of emotion. How could I be free and then thrown back into such
confusion?

Unwilling to move further from my beloved Poland, I
tried to make an agreement with God: if it were his will for
us to move to California, he'd open doors. I wasn't happy
in Massachusetts and I felt like a caged bird at my old job,
but I didn't want new things, new engineering roles, or a
new community. I wanted Poland, my Poland. I wanted to
feel free again. Like a stubborn child, I crossed my arms and
waited for signs to take tiny baby steps toward San Luis.

As with a toddler, my patient Father gave me his hand
to steady me going forward, pouring out blessing after
blessing, assuring me of his love. Andrés found me a great
company that suited my interests and skills with an immediate opening. I even had a referral connection from one
of Andrés' coworkers. My current boss was supportive of
my move and wrote a recommendation letter. The inter-
views came quickly, and they went well: I was flown to SLO
to meet the team for the final decision. A warm hug from
an administrator calmed my nerves when I arrived for my
in-person interview. I received a great offer letter and had
favorable negotiations the following day. When we moved
soon after, Andrés and I had more than a week off to road
trip together cross-country. We found a sunny apartment
within our budget and close to downtown. San Luis Obispo

was a beautiful city with surrounding foothills, begging for hikes and exploration, the ocean within view from the peaks. I watched as happy people commuted to work on bicycles.

The Lord even answered a longing in my heart from 2014 I had forgotten: I had previously told Andrés I would only move away from my family if I was plugged into a good local church that loved Jesus. Then as soon as we moved, we found a great non-denominational church, and God's love and joy were evident in the moving worship and scripture-based sermons. God even changed Andrés' heart, giving him the desire to attend with me. It was a big change of style and pace from our previous churches, but we were ready to grow together. The Lord knew my needs, he knew our family's needs, and he blessed them.

I still had an ache in my soul after we moved. Depression lingered, and I fought discouragement. Glimpses of God's love broke through my fog, but I still struggled with insecurity and shame. In my journal, I preached the gospel to myself. The Lord gave me a hand up from the depths once again.

July 22, 2017

Jesus came to heal all my hurts, disappointments, and loneliness I have carried from childhood. He dearly loved me then and loves me just as much now.

I am not my past abuse, neglect, shame, anger. I am made new. Pure. Clean. Blameless only from the power of the cross. I can't earn credit to blot out my sin and shame. Nor on the other end, do

I want to trample on what the cross truly means. If he came to set me free, I am truly free indeed!

How do I release the burdens of loneliness and brokenness from my childhood? Can I be honest with myself? Can I be open to others without getting trapped in overwhelming negative emotions? Can I stop giving my past power over my present life and believe God will be glorified as he restores all broken things, including me? Yes...

As I walked last night, I was overlooking a park with mighty green trees, swaying golden grass, and warm rays of the setting sun. A little girl with a pink shirt was rolling up and down a path on her scooter. She must have been no more than five. The golden light backlit her; she had a crown of sunshine. It was a perfect snapshot of childhood innocence and joy. God whispered to my spirit, 'I love you, precious girl, and that will be you once again. I will restore your joy and heal your pain. You will delight in me again, my beautiful daughter.' I immediately felt he had been with me all along. I knew my future would be secure, surrounded by his love.

"But for you who revere my name, the sun of righteousness will rise with healing in its rays. And you will go out and frolic like well-fed calves." Malachi 4:2

We got pregnant soon after this beautiful revelation of God's love. And we praised God I had an easy, healthy pregnancy, and I held fast to God's promise to be with me in the waters and fires of my life after Baby Orlando was born. My bump grew along with my anticipation for a new chapter in life.

But then our sweet girl, Annabelle, arrived and I was paralyzed with postpartum depression. I was numb. I was overwhelmed. I didn't see purpose or hope in anything. I couldn't get enough love from Andrés. I said awful, hurtful things to him. I felt so broken, alone, and misunderstood. How could I pray for my daughter's future when I didn't have hope for my own? I sought Christian counseling. It helped me feel less overwhelmed, less hopeless, but the depression followed like a persistent dark cloud threatening emotional storms. Trying medication seemed out of the question, I believed my season of needing it was done and felt shame for not praying hard enough. I fought with counseling, exercise, and scripture, hoping God would scoop me up once again.

After eight months of darkness, in January of 2019, I had a two-month respite. God gave me a vision. I was in a field running free covered in golden rays. Green, vibrant life surrounded me. My arms were outstretched, and I was overwhelmed with delight. I felt his joy through and through. A seed of hope was planted by the Lord—a new season was coming!

I continued to seek God and pray about my hope of spring. Rowing at the YMCA one day, the Lord stopped me dead in my tracks. *Are you walking by my Spirit?* With my depression lifted, I saw I had let my condition, feelings, and fears define me instead of my identity in Christ.

God had taught me so much in the last few years. Andrés was a new follower of Jesus (hello, praise hands!) and I felt I hadn't been a godly example for him, for Annabelle, or for my own wellbeing. I realized only I was responsible for my relationship with the Lord. My circumstances, family, and friends couldn't make me draw closer to God. I couldn't let my feelings decide if I felt God was good that day. *Forgive me, Father, for striving and ignoring the nudges from your loving Spirit.*

That night I put up a sign in our living room, "Welcome Holy Spirit" amidst my lingering Christmas garlands. (I love Christmas too much to put decor away before February).

And he came rushing in with new hope!

Over the next few weeks, God spoke into my life. What he had planted in my heart sprouted and was finally ready to bud. I started writing this book about my beloved Poland. "A Walk in the Forest" flowed out of my pen like a ceaseless stream. I was transported to my beautiful Polish beech trees stretching out before me and God's presence beckoning me. He gave me a new spring delighting in his presence.

Then days after I began writing, I received a message from a sweet, wise friend, Kerin. She had no idea about my traumatic past, nor my transformational season in Poland. But the Lord knew. It was a beautiful confirmation of the new blossoms to come.

> *"You are a priceless treasure in your Father God's heart. He knows how the touch you received from his Spirit has set you apart, and he is aware of the cost of being set apart. It's favor, really. He has such compassion toward you and treasures your 'yes.' Now it's as if, with a twinkle in his eye, he is leaning forward and fanning the flame he set in you with his very breath. He knows you so well and loves you dearly."*

(Cue the breakthrough cry.)

From my winters, I knew the Lord's voice much more intimately. I was wiser and believed in his power to restore broken, lost things, including me. I wrote and wrote. I wrote for my soul to remember. His love surrounded me as a melody woven through my story. Healing tears often fell onto the pages of my Bible and keyboard. I was undone by fresh revelations of his loving-kindness. So much so, I used "tender" 46 times in the first draft of my manuscript. Friend, I want you to know the profound love of Father God for *you*. My heart aches for you to know it in your bones and heart of hearts.

Although my depression came back, I fought the enemy's lies and continued to write. In May of 2019, I found a passage about the bleeding woman in the gospel of John. If only she could touch the hem of Jesus' garment, she believed she would be healed. I was in awe of her bold trust. I had had enough with my depression. I proclaimed to my friends at Bible study I was done, and God was going to heal me! Psalm 40 burst out of my mouth.

I waited patiently for the Lord;
he turned to me and heard my cry.
He lifted me out of the slimy pit,
out of the mud and mire;
he set my feet on a rock and
gave me a firm place to stand.
Psalm 40:1-2

The next morning, I woke to the sun streaming in my room. His light was aglow within me. My heaviness was gone; as if I had never known its weight. His deep peace covered me and tears of joy spilled down my cheeks. My depression, praise God, didn't return. One week, then two, then a month, and the depression stayed away. My friends and I praised Jesus every time they asked how I was feeling and saw it hadn't returned.

For the last eight months, I have rejoiced in my spring. I have been writing out my heart and am continuing to experience God's powerful presence in new and exciting ways. I constantly run after Jesus, letting him fill me with the fullness of his love, and delightfully pouring it into lonely, broken people. I desperately want everyone to know and experience the love that profoundly changed my life. If I could, I'd bear hug you, then grab you by the shoulders, looking you square in the eye and tell you, "This hope is for *you.*"

Through and through, I know only his precious love could reshape my heart and set me on a new path of profound purpose. The perfect love of my Father, who knows me, created me, and loves me completely. Whether in winter, spring, or any season, God promises he can be found. Believing he wants to be with me and delights in me, is my most precious gift. He is the lover of my broken soul, and I have nothing to hide. I wait expectantly for the day I am completely restored, drawn in close to his heart, and see the love in his eyes face to face. I catch a glimpse in my mind, "Sarah, from now on I will call you *Beautiful Hope.*"

"For I know the plans I have for you," declares the Lord, "plans to prosper you and not to harm you, plans to give you hope and a future. Then you will call on me and come and pray to me, and I will listen to you. You will seek me and find me when you seek me with all your heart. I will be found by

you," declares the Lord, "and I will bring you back from captivity. I will gather you from all the nations and places where I have banished you," declares the Lord, "and will bring you back to the place from which I carried you into exile." Jeremiah 29:11-14

God's hands are in all parts of my life. He carried me into the hard places yet has been faithful to deliver me. Whether I'm in awful suffering, or great joy, my life is nothing if I didn't have the power of God's love encircling me. I couldn't imagine my life without my suffering. The hardest times have been a fire to refine my heart and set me on a path to earnestly seek my Father. Pain enabled me to know from the depths of my soul, there was more to the suffering of this life. There was something to quiet the ache in my heart, begging for love. And I found it in Poland:

Jesus.

After finding him, and learning his heart, I couldn't run anywhere else. And so I step into trials, struggles, knowing Jesus is with me, shaping my heart to be like his. I rest in his grace knowing he loves me as I am, as I struggle, seek, grow, and trust him. He is not afraid of my whole story.

Jesus is by my side, delighting in the green shoots and providing for me and my family. He has shown his steadfast character by carrying us through so much, including our debt payoff, despite my valleys of depression. Four years and ten months after we started our debt-free journey, our last payment was made in February 2020. We're debt-free!

The yoke of debt no longer enslaves us. In the end, with ridiculously frustrating interest, we paid $278,964.76.

It feels surreal. We can do hard things through Christ! We worked as a team. We prayed. We cried (OK, I was the big crier). We stuck to our plan and the Lord honored our diligence. It was hard, but I wouldn't want it any other way. We worked for it, sacrificed a lot of conveniences and comforts, and our hearts were changed in the process. Conquering mountains of debt fuels my hope for future challenges as a family and trusting God to guide and provide a way to grow and stretch us.

> *Consider it joy, brothers and sisters, when you face trials of many kinds, because you know that the testing of your faith produces perseverance. Let perseverance finish its work so that you may be mature and complete, not lacking anything.* James 1:2-4

I don't believe I will see all his promises on this side of heaven. I know trials and sorrow will come. I know I can't be completely delivered from sin and suffering here on Earth. Some things will happen I won't understand. But now I have tasted and seen the Lord's goodness. I have found rest for my soul, trusting in his goodness, faithfulness, and sovereignty. He has loved me and always will.

Yes, Jesus, I don't want anything else but to dwell in your love.

My Jesus will always be working for my good and drawing me closer to his heart. I am only at the beginning of a beautiful journey. On the top of a mountain the locals call "Madonna" I penned a reflection and prayer on suffering and sin.

186

Rain washed away the dirt, pebbles, and all else, exposing the solid rock below. Removing the shakable and leaving only that which can't be shaken; that is Christ. [25]

I have been climbing "Mount Injury," (an idea from Hinds Feet on High Places), I admit I have hurt myself, I have hurt others, and I have been hurt.[26] *I didn't deserve the pain of another's sin, yet I suffered. Nor did others deserve to suffer from my sin.*

But then I recalled my Advent scriptures from today.[27] *Jesus was crushed for my sin—for everyone's sin—he didn't deserve it, but he submitted to his Father, so we may be healed. Because he loved us too much to leave us in darkness.*

I want to submit to suffering as it makes me more like Christ. In my crushing, I want his aroma to be streaming out of me as I bear my challenges and trials.

I want to forgive myself and forgive others for the sins that deeply wounded me. Higher places will remain but a faint horizon if I continue limping in these injuries, wearing battle scars of "abuser" and "victim" and "unlovable." The healing process hurts, but it is far better than being stuck in the valley of despair forever.

I have hope for my redemption story.

"Love and Pain go together, for a time at least," the Shepherd gently told Much-Afraid in Hinds Feet on High Places. [28] Letting the Shepherd, Jesus, love means being vulnerable and honest with the state of my broken heart. Loving others means I may get hurt and be rejected, but I can choose to love anyway, unafraid. I can choose to speak the truth with love and share the encouragement God has given me. Or I can keep it to myself and hide it, afraid I will disappoint the Lord. [29]

I have been given much and want to feed the sheep Christ has given me to lead. I can only because Christ loves me more.

As clay in your hands, Lord, you are shaping my beautiful heart.

Let me be soft to your touch, submitting to your will and unimaginable master plan for my life. I want to display your beauty, the unique expression of your heart, as an image-bearer, stamped, and sealed with your Spirit. May others know you as they see you radiate through me.

I am nothing apart from your love and faithfulness.

Take out all my impurities, wash me, cleanse me, and I will be clean.

None of my hope is apart from the goodness of Jesus working in my heart, relentlessly pursuing me with his love, and bringing me into a secure relationship with him. He loved me enough to die on a cross to redeem my sinful, broken heart. In Poland, I finally stopped running from his love. I stopped trying to earn my worth. I stopped living in shame and believing my worst sins were unforgivable. But I was only able to trust and receive his grace after I fell apart and invited him into my pain, trusting his extravagant love for me.

Writing this book has helped me remember and solidify what God spoke to me in Poland about who I am and who he is. He demolished limiting beliefs, false gospels, and fears that held me captive. I have been drawn close to Jesus, and his healing hand, I would never turn anywhere else. In God's beautiful rhythm of grace, as I have given you a piece of my heart, in turn, God has filled me increasingly with his.

I pray these love letters speak to your weary, broken heart. You, too, are about to claim a new story—a story of restoration and hope. I pray you embrace your tender walk with the Lord. Be surprised by his goodness. Get your hopes up, friend! He is calling you to an abundant life, a life of freedom, hope, and unshakable love. Do you know that kind of love? I hope you do, especially after reading my story. No, I am not a special woman, just a redeemed and loved woman, who wants to share how Jesus' love transforms lives. His heart is to pursue and transform all his children, including you, my friend.

As you claim and walk out your new identity, I would love to rejoice with you and hear your freedom songs with good coffee, hugs, tears, and cozy couches. I pray Christ may dwell richly in your heart and you may know in the depths of your thirsty soul how wide and long and high and deep is the love of Christ for you.

He lifted me out of the pit of despair,
out of the mud and the mire.
He set my feet on solid ground
and steadied me as I walked along.
He has given me a new song to sing,
a hymn of praise to our God.
Many will see what he has done and be amazed.
They will put their trust in the Lord.
Psalm 40:2-3 NLT

My sweet family and I went to New England for Christmas just weeks after my mountaintop reflection. It was the first time I went back East since I started writing my story. We drove up the little hill, past the white farmhouse, and around the bend onto the familiar road lined with pines. It was the first time my precious daughter, Annabelle, made the trip too. I was burdened by a deep desire to preserve her innocence and protect her delicate heart. And my wise counselor's advice came to mind, "Your past is not her past. She doesn't have your memories." With a deep breath, I released those feelings to God and prayed, *let me trust you with her story.*

But then I struggled with my own memories, trying to remind myself I wasn't a little girl anymore, feeling lost and unloved. Or I wasn't a quietly rebellious, broken teenager seeking love in the wrong places. No, I was a new creation. *I know who I am.*

Therefore, if anyone is in Christ, the new creation has come. The old has gone, the new is here! 2 Corinthians 5:17

190

We drove down a country road I had been on thousands of times. But this time was different. Just before the bridge over the Contoocook River, a pine forest hugged the riverbanks and wintery hills.

I looked out and caught my breath; quiet tears flowed. Andrés and my sister carried on with the conversation, unaware of the deep work in my heart as the Lord tenderly reminded me of who I was.

Through the evergreens, the sunset danced on fresh snow, making each flake sparkle, brilliant white. *It reflected me.*

Beautiful.

Forgiven.

His beloved daughter.

Acknowledgments

To my loving Father who kept pursuing my sensitive heart and brought me on this path of restoration and freedom. May I always adore you and give honor for every good thing.

Andrés, babe, thank you for your unfailing love and carving out time for me to write on weekends, at nap time, and other slivers of time in our busy days. You have continually encouraged me to write my story and to find deeper freedom in Jesus. I appreciate your heart to serve with perfectly timed prayers, bottomless cups of tea, shoulder rubs, and making space for me to thrive. I love you mucho.

Megan Thomas, I am grateful for your beautiful heart and inquisitive mind as you edited my manuscript. As iron sharpens iron, you have helped me invite the reader into the deeper story within. Thank you for your wisdom, research, and prayerful ponderings to understand my heart and help me share it with my readers.

Thank you, Cutie Pie, for being a supporter, editor, and cheerleader for my story to be shared. Thanks for the last-minute FaceTime editing and laughing about word choice reasons to use "fart." I am grateful for your insights, humor, and forever friendship. Cue the Grease song, "We go together." I love you bunches.

Kari, thank you for your sweet, prayerful spirit and your godly insights and blessings over my first complete draft of the manuscript. I will always treasure our sunny afternoon together reviewing my work and praying.

Thank you, Susan Boyd, you were the first to listen to the catalyst for my book: "A Walk in the Forest," after helping me outline the book with creative chapter titles. You have given me the courage to keep sharing with the metaphors the Lord gives me. You have been a sounding board for understanding the mechanics of writing a book and how to navigate the big world of publishing.

Gosia, I am grateful for your friendship and laughter. Thank you for introducing me to Polish hip-hop, Polish Gospel music, and many other wonderful things. Thank you for translating this manuscript and your kind words of encouragement throughout the past four years as I've grown to know Jesus' heart even deeper.

Thank you, Pastors Marek and Ala, for welcoming me into your church community and home as one of your own. Thank you for your hospitality, blessings, and continued prayers. You introduced me to the true Rivers of the Living Water, Jesus, and for that, I am eternally grateful.

Thank you, Rafi and Katie, for the belly laughs and for encouraging me to try new challenges. Thanks for starting the "Meow Meow" Whatsapp group. Thank you, Katie, for being my first real friend I did life with and welcoming me into your heart and home. I still miss that little rascal, Stella, and her spunk.

Thank you, Grammie "That Sews", for reading my draft manuscript in its entirety and seeing into my heart and then sharing yours. I'll be forever grateful for our loving conversation.

To my "B-stud" gals—past and present—who have sipped tea on my couches, talked about Jesus and laughed together. Thank you for your constant encouragement and hugs. I'm grateful for a safe place to share my victories and frustrations of authoring my story. You are all an answer to prayer, my sisters.

Angie, thank you for being you and encouraging me to "get curious" to past limiting beliefs and reaching for all the Lord has for my heart. I am slowly realizing his plan is more amazing and beautiful than I could ever ask or imagine. I will always treasure our first conversation together and you said, "do you hear yourself?! You sound *free*." And the new freedom I've found is because of the Lord working through you.

Thank you to Mum, Iulia, Megan Omli, Molly Dunn, Alyssa Howarter, Joanna Jezierska, Chloe Murray, Cierra Irwin, Lorin Stockle, Loryn Bourquin, Brooke Jeffrey, Brooke Clare, Kerin Clement, and Alexis Bynum many others for reading excerpts and first drafts of my book and speaking life to me. You spurred me to keep writing and sharing my story.

I keep asking that the God of our Lord Jesus Christ, the glorious Father, may give you the spirit of wisdom and revelation, so that you may know him better. Ephesians 1:17

Sources

Chapter 2:

1. John 10:10.

2. Priscilla Shirer, *Gideon: Your Weakness. God's STRENGTH*, (Nashville, TN: Lifeway, 2015).

3. Psalm 118:5.

4. Zephaniah 3:17.

5. Zig Ziglar, "Self-Talk Christian Affirmation Card," Ziglar Inc.© 2020 Choose to Win, October 21, 2020, https://mk0ziglar4ifu5ixq7cx.kinstacdn.com/wp-content/uploads/2019/03/Choose-to-Win-Self-Talk-Card-Christian.pdf.

6. 1 Corinthians 1:27.

Chapter 5:

7. "Gospel," Encyclopedia Britannica, Oct 30, 2020, https://www.britannica.com/topic/Gospel-New-Testament.

8. "The Gospel of Caesar Augustus, & What It Tells Us About the Gospel of Jesus Christ," Nick Cady Longmont Pastor, November 22, 2020, https://nickcady.org/2019/01/09/the-gospel-of-caesar-augustus-what-it-tells-us-about-the-gospel-of-jesus-christ.

9. Matthew 5:3-10.

10. "Gospel word study," The Bible Project, October 30, 2020, https://bibleproject.com/explore/ gospel-word-study.

11. Matthew 20:16.

12. Luke 4:14-21.

13. "Immanuel," Dictionary.com, December 8, 2020, https://www.dictionary.com/browse/immanuel?s=t.

Chapter 6:

14. "DSM-5 Criteria for PTSD," Brainline, October 25, 2020, https://www.brainline.org/article/dsm-5-criteria-ptsd/.

15. National Suicide Prevention Lifeline, October 25, 2020, https://suicidepreventionlifeline.org.

SOURCES

Chapter 7:

16. "The Womb of God?" The Bible Project, October 25, 2020, https://bibleproject.com/podcast/the-womb-of-god.

Chapter 8:

17. Sermon by Pastor Marek Siudek, September 11, 2016, Słupsk, Poland, Rivers of the Living Water Christian Centre, used by permission.

Chapter 9:

18. Psalm 139:14.

Chapter 11:

19. "Weed," Dictionary.com, November 6, 2020, https://www.dictionary.com/browse/weed?s=t.

20. Mark 4:30-32.

21. John 21.

22. "Repentance," Bible Study Tools, November 16, 2020, https://www.biblestudytools.com/dictionary/repentance.

Chapter 14:

23. John 10:10.

Sources

Chapter 15:

24. Lyrics from "Because Of Your Love" lyrics, Jesus Culture Music, © Capitol CMG Genesis.

Epilogue:

25. Hebrews 12:26-29.

26. Hannah Hurnard, *Hinds Feet on High Places*, (Blacksburg, VA: Wilder, 2010), 64.

27. A verse from *Advent 2019: A Thrill of Hope*, She Reads Truth, (Quote from CSV Bible, Isaiah 53:2-12), (Nashville, TN: She Reads Truth, 2019), 67.

28. Hannah Hurnard, *Hinds Feet on High Places*, (Blacksburg, VA: Wilder, 2010), 10.

29. Matthew 25:14-30.

Additional

Resources

Ready for more hope and stories from Sarah? Check out her blog at www.sarahdeorlando.com/blog or scan the QR code below.

You may also send her a message with the QR code below. She'd love to hear how her story impacted your heart.

Grab downloadable Love Letters from Poland discussion questions and fun other freebies with the following QR code or at www.sarahdeorlando.com/love-letters-bonus.

Visiting northern Poland and want to check out a great church? Or do you want to learn more about the construction of the Rivers of Living Water Christian Centre? Visit their website: http://ccrwz.pl/en.

Notes

Notes

Sarah de Orlando Coaching

Sarah de Orlando the Chief-Hope-Giver and Founder of Sarah de Orlando Coaching. Her heart is to help women gain confidence, overcome fear, and live the purposeful life God designed uniquely for them through coaching, speaking, and writing.

She guides women through a proven process to help you conquer fear and overwhelm so you move forward and ultimately transform your life, one simple habit at a time.

She has been where you are. She has been filled with self-doubt, stuck, and wondering if she was enough. But she is here to tell you there is hope for you to grow and thrive! As a licensed Choose to Win Coach through Ziglar, Sarah loves teaching with biblical truth to transform the lives of women. Join her community as you take your first brave step into your dreams!

Contact Sarah with the code below to learn more about:

- Joining her private Facebook community
- Small group coaching
- One-on-one coaching
- Speaking inquiries